Career Guidance
for Now
and for the Future

RCIS

Resumés, Cover Letters & Interviews lead to Your SUCCESS

Career Guidance
for Now
and for the Future

RCI Program to Success

Melissa Hume

BALBOA
PRESS
A DIVISION OF HAY HOUSE

Balboa Press books may be ordered through booksellers or by contacting:

Balboa Press
A Division of Hay House
1663 Liberty Drive
Bloomington, IN 47403
www.balboapress.com.au
1 (877) 407-4847

Printed in the United States of America.

ISBN: 978-1-4525-2558-7 (sc)
ISBN: 978-1-4525-2559-4 (e)

Balboa Press rev. date: 09/22/2014

A special thank you to my twin sister, Amy. Thank you for your love, constructive criticism, and continual encouragement during the entire writing and publishing process.

Contents

Preface

I've been asked a number of times why I started RCI Success. I give the same answer every time: people need help! I cannot tell you the number of friends, family, and various individuals whom are struggling to find work. Especially now. This economic climate is proving to be tough for many, and a lot do not realise that finding a job is not easy ... unless you know the processes inside and out.

Résumé writing, cover letter writing, and acing an interview all take time to perfect. The good news is, your learning can be fast-tracked! In early 2013 I recognised a void in the market for help with this; no one else was helping. And so a couple of months later, RCI Success was spawned. I began developing one-on-one coaching sessions which break down the steps to securing a job quickly. They cover CVs, cover letters, interview tips, and techniques, and they provide insights into employer perspectives and how recruitment agencies operate. From this, I developed workshops which educate large audiences in an interactive manner.

As the owner of RCI Success, I hope to help others, and by doing so to be rewarded myself. So that's my story.

If you are looking for a job, do not give up. Keep trying, and soon employers will see the value in who you are as a person and what you can offer their organisation.

Introduction

About RCI Success

RCI Success is a *proudly Australian-owned business* established in NSW by Melissa Hume. Using RCI Success as her vehicle, Melissa has built a reputation for adding value to individuals' résumés and cover letters, increasing candidate confidence during telephone and one-on-one interviews, and significantly increasing the likelihood of landing an ideal job.

Areas of expertise:

- Résumé writing and structure
- Cover letters
- Interview behaviour and etiquette
- Job application process
- Enlightenment in areas of recruitment and the processes involved in being placed as a job candidate
- Delivering a psychological perspective on areas of employment

Why RCI Success Services Are Different

Unlike workshops held by education bodies and recruitment agencies, our coaching sessions are one-on-one. Sessions will answer *your* questions, and they are thereby directed by *you*. Workshops include a psychological perspective and deliver what might be dry content in an interesting way.

We listen first and then teach. With the mindset that job hunting is a lifelong skill, sessions teach you what *you* want to learn to help you now and for the future.

RCI Success services are recommended for the following clients:

- University graduates looking to get their foot in the door
- Undergraduates trying to land their first internship or job in their desired career industry
- High school students looking for a casual and/or part-time job and seeking to gain work experience
- Anyone looking for a career change
- Anyone who is returning to the workforce after a long absence
- Anyone finding it very difficult to "get their foot in the door"

What This RCI Success Program Covers

The aim of this book is to give an all-round understanding of how to secure employment following various steps. Recruitment and selection processes have advanced and follow structured policies and procedures. These start with filtering through résumés, analysing cover letters, and conducting interviews. RCI Success focuses on enlightening our clients on these processes. In this way, we strive to increase our clients' success in securing a job and employment for now and for the future.

This program also ventures beyond basic employment strategies, providing a psychological perspective and guidance to employers on how to find the "right' candidate for a position. Other areas include being your own boss, a breakdown of what's expected when you begin a new job, and whether a new position is right for you.

Clients are encouraged to visit RCI Success's website for further information or to attend a specialist workshop on what they struggle with the most: résumés, cover letters, interviews, etc.

Complete the exercises at your own pace. You're encouraged to engage RCI Success's services via a one-on-one coaching session or workshop, in which you can discuss your progress or any areas you believe you require improvement on.

The Program's Structure

This program is broken into areas in which RCI Success specialises:

- **R**ésumés
- **C**over Letters
- **I**nterviews
- Strategies for **SUCCESS**

Further Information

If you have questions regarding this program, please feel free to raise an enquiry with RCI Success at info@rcisuccess.com.au.

Please visit http://rcisuccess.com.au, or interact with Melissa via her blog at http://rcisuccess.net.

Chapter 1

A Step-by-Step Guide for Job Applications

This chapter will introduce you to the basic steps and strategies you can use to find a job. They have been proven to be effective by my clients and me.

Be Selective

Choose ten jobs and ten jobs only. Research the job descriptions. Determine how competitive the salary offered for each job is in comparison to current market trends. Analyse the potential for career progression and each company's growth by reading public annual reports and reading news of its recent product or service launches. Each job must be one in which you see yourself prospering, and it must be within an organisation you would love to work for. Conducting research first is key! Now that you've done your research …

Print Out Each Job You've Applied To

Print off the advertisements for the ten jobs you've chosen. Shrink the advertisements so that the full job description (JD) is on one page. On the printout, note the date you made your application and the name of the person responsible for the recruitment and selection process.

Carry these printouts around with you at all times. This will ensure that if an HR staff person or recruitment consultant contacts you regarding your application, you will always be prepared. You will be more than able to mention specific aspects of the position's responsibilities, main performance targets, and the company itself which captured your attention and motivated you to apply.

Using the printout as a guide, you will not sound like you've been applying to anything and everything. The impression you will project is that this is the only job you have applied for, as you are able to "recall" specific details. The printouts will give your conversation structure, will help you be enthusiastic, and will limit the amount of *ums* and *uhs* you say—not to mention that quoting aspects of the JD is quite impressive.

Application Process

If you continuously apply for jobs with no success, you need to take a step back and determine what part or parts of your application are letting you down.

- *Need/want recognition*—You know what type of job you want, and you are keen to progress to the interview stage.
- *Job search*—What mediums are you using? Are you limiting yourself to only one website, or are you utilising all possible sources?
- *Evaluations of options*—What is the most successful approach, considering time and resources available?
- *Applying to the job*—Are you including a specifically tailored cover letter? Are you presenting yourself professionally in the email you write and over the telephone?

Post-application evaluation—Is your approach working? Do you need to rethink one of your application stages?

If you keep using the same strategy to no avail, you cannot expect a different result. Although it may be difficult, you need to consider that your CV is not selling your skills and experience effectively. This may be the case if you keep applying to jobs and receive no or little response. If you make it to the interview stage and do not progress, perhaps others are perceiving you in a way you do not intend.

Whatever stage you're struggling with, realising the faults in your application process is necessary for job placement. Success can start only when you are being open to self-criticism and improvement.

Writing an Email to a Recruitment Agency or Potential Employer

If you prefer to or are advised by the job advertisement to apply directly to a specified email address, the email you write must be professional. Short and simple is best.

Ensure grammar and punctuation are correct. And also thank the contact person by name for his or her consideration, and indicate that you look forward to discussing opportunities with him or her. Also insert a signature consistent with the body of text, as in the example below.

> *Good afternoon, Lily,*
>
> *This email is an expression of my interest regarding the Marketing Internship currently advertised on SEEK.*
>
> *Please find my CV attached for your perusal.*
>
> *Please contact me on 0407-199-382 at your earliest convenience to discuss this position further.*
>
> *Thank you for your consideration.*
>
> *Regards,*
>
> *Melanie Fiest*
>
> *M: 0407-199-382*
>
> *E: Melanie.fiest58@yahoo.com.au*

Writing a Follow-up Email after a Phone Call

A follow-up email needs to demonstrate your enthusiasm towards the advertised role without being pushy and without demanding information about employer's selection or application progress. With this in mind, your call must be short and polite. You should send this email if you haven't been contacted after submitting your CV and cover letter.

> *Dear Bob,*
>
> *I'm enquiring about the progress you've made towards the HR assistant position.*
>
> *I'm quite enthusiastic about the role and would like the opportunity to present myself in an interview if the position has not yet been filled.*
>
> *I look forward to your response.*
>
> *Yours Sincerely,*
> *Melanie Humack*

Other Application Strategies

Get in contact with recruitment consultants which have interviewed you and were unable to place you. Remind them of the position you came close to being chosen for. You need to demonstrate your continued interest in working with them. Since they've interviewed you previously, they know how well you present yourself, the competencies and skills you possess, and what work environment would best suit you. Use these as a selling point for them to find you a job placement. Don't forget that they make a commission if they're successful!

Networking

When you go for interviews, keep every business card you are given and store these in a folder for safekeeping. You can contact these recruitment consultants in the future regarding job interviews. Keep the cards associated with positive interviews only. You can still keep them even if you are not placed in a position. Discard any business cards associated with negative interviews.

Also utilise social media websites to connect with people in your chosen industry or job role. Further information on networking is available in a later chapter of this book.

Understanding and Practicing Selection Tests

Many companies and recruitment agencies use selection tools such as psychological, numerical, and intelligence tests to differentiate between weak and strong candidates for a job position. Preparation before being examined is fundamental to increasing your chances of passing or excelling on one of these tests.

Practise tests are rarely available. However, journal articles, forums, and websites provide valuable information on what to expect and what information about you is being gleaned from each question. Research such as this is great preparation. Simple, free practise tests for typing speed and Microsoft programs (Word, Excel, and PowerPoint) can be found on the Internet. Preparation guides are also available for numerical comprehension, verbal comprehension, and error checking tests.

Applying Directly to Jobs

With an increasingly competitive market and soaring unemployment rates, seldom will you find advertisements managed and controlled directly by the hiring organisation. Internal recruitment is becoming rare and is being overtaken by recruitment agencies. Outsourced recruitment activities create difficulty in applying directly to an organisation, especially if direct contact information is not available.

The advantages of applying directly to the hiring organisation include the following:

1. You bypass recruitment consultants, who act as the first filter. They are often riddled with personal biases. After engaging with numerous candidates, they usually form a stereotype of what an ideal candidate will look and behave like. If you do not conform to this stereotype, you can be rejected despite having competencies suitable for the job. Recruitment consultants also do not have an in-depth understanding of every client's industry, the organisation's culture, or the needs which must be fulfilled by the right candidate.

2. Interviews conducted by internal HR personnel tend to provide more information regarding their company and their expectations, and clearer descriptions of the job and work environment. Recruitment consultants, on the other hand, are bound by confidentiality agreements, so they are unable to disclose information until they are sure a candidate has a good chance of being well received by their client. Liaising directly with internal HR personnel makes it substantially easier for you, as the candidate, to determine if this is the type of organisation you can see yourself working for. It is also an opportunity to gain answers to questions regarding opportunities for career progression, how the organisation is structured internally, who you will be reporting to, and what the boss is like. External bodies cannot answer these questions.

3. Any recruitment consultant's ultimate goal is to fill a position and earn a commission-based fee for the placement. As the candidate, you act as the means to receiving this commission. It is then fair to say that most consultants do not have the candidate's best interests in mind; satisfying their client is their primary focus. Ascertaining whether the placement will benefit the candidate in

terms of career progression, monetary gain, and intrinsic value is commonly ignored. However, HR managers make the candidate's attitude and "fit" in the company a priority, as they understand the internal ramifications for both the client and the candidate if the wrong candidate is chosen. Ramifications can range from intellectual and property threat, damage to the organisation's reputation through intentional error or incompetence, financial loss from termination of employment, profit loss via customer complaints, and disruption to the organisational culture.

4. When companies seek a pool of candidates outside their company, they are searching for people who can add value to their company. It is well known that excessive reliance on internal promotion and recruitment results in employee cloning; the same ideas and skills are recycled. This has the potential to stunt the organisation's growth and available expertise, particularly in small organisations. Therefore, HR managers often seek employees who are untainted by their industry, have relevant experience, and are able to bring with them new expertise and ideas. Keep this in mind if your career is taking a new direction. When they ask you why they should choose you over other candidates, pitch the following:

    •   You can offer different expertise and experience.
    •   Your previous work experience, skills, and knowledge are transferable to the job vacancy.
    •   You'd add diversity to the organisation (if they are a small business).

Cold Job Applications

Apply directly to organisations which you have researched and have an interest in working for, despite seeing no advertisements or having no knowledge of position vacancies. You can do this in an email format or by approaching them directly. This is covered in depth in another chapter of this book.

Here is an example of a cold email:

(Mark your email as important with an exclamation point, using Outlook.)

Subject: *I would love to work for you!*

> *Good morning, Barry,*
>
> *I would love the opportunity to work for you!*
>
> *I've researched [company name] and feel as though I could offer your organisation and your team expertise on your new product launch project.*
>
> *As a current Project Manager at [company name], I've personally organised and ensured the success of our own product X launch. I've recognised that your [product name] has the potential to grow and prosper rapidly, especially with the [brief details of product, current market research, and competitor analysis].*
>
> *I've attached my CV for your perusal.*
>
> *Please contact me on 0407-199-382 at your earliest convenience to discuss position opportunities.*
>
> *Thank you for your time.*
>
> *Regards,*
>
> *[full name]*
>
> *Mobile*
>
> *Email*

Walk-in Approach

A walk-in approach is, in one word, proactive! Confidence, practise, and the right strategy are required to execute it well. Further guidance on this approach is provided in a later chapter of this book, but an introduction follows.

The first step involves printing off multiple copies of your résumé and presenting it personally to potential employers. You should request to speak to the person who internally recruits, HR, or the business owner, depending on the size and structure of the organisation you approach.

Remember that first impressions truly do matter. You must dress appropriately, in accordance with the type of role you're applying for. For example, if you're applying for an accountancy position, dress in a suit.

Be confident and ask direct, concise questions. Elaborate upon your experiences. Be sure to use the jargon of the business correctly when you converse with the contact person.

Chapter 2

Résumés

Your résumé is the first impression you give to a potential employer or recruitment consultant. It needs to market your skills, qualifications, and experience in a way that suits the particular job you are applying for. Therefore, a résumé should be treated as the first layer of your overall selling pitch. It must be specifically tailored to each job you apply for—in content and in format.

Great résumés take a lot of time to write and edit. Do not assume that résumé writing is easy and that your first draft is sufficient.

General Rules for Formatting

Remember that different people are going to view your résumé. You need to choose a font size suitable for people with poor vision. I recommend using 11- or 12-point Times New Roman or Calibri, as these are the standard for CVs.

Your résumé must be easy on the eyes. Bullet points, paragraphs, and lines must be consistently aligned and pleasant to glance over. Anything that is messy and requires effort can irritate the reader, who might dismiss your résumé despite its relevant content.

Include appropriate information about each previous job. Highlight any important responsibilities, features of your role, or achievements.

Number the pages of résumé for the readers' use. On each page, leave margins sufficient enough for readers to write comments when they print out your résumé. Note taking is a common practise of recruitment consultants and employers.

Check all documents with spellcheck and grammar. Also manually check your document for errors and ensure that paragraphs make sense. Review your document at least two times before applying.

Language

Avoid colloquialisms in your résumé. Emphasise your level of professionalism by substituting colloquial phrases with strong descriptive statements—for example, "liaised with clients," "consulted with clients," or "negotiated with clients" are professional substitutes for "talked to clients."

Do not use jargon you do not understand. Using these in the wrong context can be detrimental to your application's success.

Content

Avoid content which can cause an employer or recruitment consultant to discriminate against you and limit your chances of progressing to the interview stage. Content which should be excluded from your résumé includes the following:

- Address
- Age/date of birth
- Gender (although your name is normally an indicator)
- Year you graduated from high school or completed your school certificate (employers can use this to estimate your age)
- Marital status
- Personal photos (research indicates that interviewers are more favourable towards good-looking candidates and ignore their less attractive counterparts despite equal experience, qualifications, and/or skills)

Reducing the amount of personal information available on your CV protects you from identity theft in the chance that you accidentally apply to a scam job.

Résumé Checklist

Use this checklist to ensure your CV is to a high standard. Complete it before submitting your CV for jobs.

- ☐ Contact details:
- ☐ State your full name and contact details in an easy-to-read font.
- ☐ Make sure your email is underlined and highlighted in blue (hyperlinked).
- ☐ Double-check your contact details.

Career objective/summary:

- ☐ Your career objective must be relevant to the position you apply for.
- ☐ It indicates what industry you want to develop your career in, your long-term career goals, how you would like to apply your degree to your career, etc.

Education:

- ☐ Include the full name of your degree, the name of the institution, the finish date or estimated finish date.
- ☐ Show your academic achievements.
- ☐ Mention your GPA if it's necessary for the application or is quite high.

Professional memberships:

- ☐ Name any organisations or associations in which you have a membership, such as AHRI, APS, CPA Australia, or Psychology Society.
- ☐ Indicate your level of membership, and include the year you started your membership.

☐ If you are not a part of any organisations, strongly consider becoming a member in an association linked to your industry. Membership shows your intent to excel in your career and a genuine interest in your industry.

Employment:

☐ List your skills and knowledge. Bullet points are recommended.
☐ Highlight any major achievements or projects you were responsible for or involved in.
☐ Use past tense and first person.
☐ Avoid passive verbs. Use active verbs.

Volunteer/extracurricular activities:

☐ Provide evidence of your transferable skills.
☐ Highlight any experience relevant for the current position.
☐ Give examples of your level of involvement.

Travel:

☐ Include overseas work or study that demonstrates your level of confidence.

Referees:

☐ Consider showing or excluding your referees on your CV. This is a personal choice.
☐ Referees should not be family or friends; they must be superiors from your previous or current employment.
☐ Brief your referees about the type of position you're seeking so they can give professional and positive references.

The Top Ten Résumés Mistakes

Australia's unemployment rates are increasing. Jobs are scarce, so there are substantially more people searching for jobs than there are jobs available.

With this competition, you need to stand out. As your first point of contact, your CV is the most crucial step in the job acquisition process. Below are ten of the most common mistakes people make on their CVs.

1. If your CV is filled with grammatical and spelling errors, this is a major mistake. Spellcheck, edit, and reedit. Your résumé is what gives an employer a first impression of you, and first impressions are hard to change. A CV riddled with errors suggests that you don't care enough to edit and make your work presentable and accurate. It also indicates that you are not serious about the job offer, as you could not muster the effort to check your CV. If you find it difficult to spot errors or are not a perfectionist by nature, ask a friend to look over it.

2. Think of your CV as a blank canvass. Using words, paint a clear picture of who you are in terms of your experiences, knowledge, qualifications, and personality. You have only one canvas, so your CV must be specific, concise, and relevant to the job advertised.

3. Tailor your CV to every job you apply to. It is useful to have a general template so that you don't neglect important pieces of information, but the mindset that "one CV suits all" is naïve and detrimental to your job search.

4. Your CV should focus on the duties, responsibilities, and key achievements in your current and previous jobs. Try not to focus on the outcomes, but on how you worked in a team or individually to reach those outcomes.

5. Your CV should not be long. Employers are busy people; sometimes they have hundreds of CVs to filter through. Although brevity is the soul of a CV, neglecting vital information is not conducive to your job search. Finding a balance between CV length and important information is a challenge, but it is very important.

6. When a candidate makes negative comments about his previous or current employer, the potential employer wonders, *If I hire him, what will he say about me and my organisation?* These attitudes can be revealed by negative phrases or sentences in CVs. Avoid this by using only positive language in your CV. If you struggle, ask someone unaware of your attitudes to analyse your paragraphs and try to discern your opinion about each former employer.

7. As mentioned above, your word choices create a sense of who you are. The employer gets the impression that you are proactive, energetic, and highly motivated if you use active sentence constructions in your role descriptions. Passive sentences give the impression that you have a laissez-faire approach or you were not very involved in or enthusiastic about your job responsibilities.

8. Use the job advertisement to guide what you highlight in your CV. Just remember not to exclude important information which demonstrates your skill sets, as many advertisements do not include the soft skills they require.

9. Ensure that your contact information is easy to find and correct.

10. Again, make sure your CV is organised, insightful, and an easy read. Be consistent with the font size and layout.

Indicators of Résumé Fraud

When you write the content of your résumé, be truthful. Inconsistencies between what you've written and what you communicate over the phone or during the interview stage will show that you have lied. This can tarnish your reputation as a prospective employee. It could also make you sound competent for a job role in which you are not suited, and if you land the job and are unable to perform, you are at the risk of being let go. You will also affect the organisation's productivity and incur additional costs, as they have to find a new employee to replace you.

To keep yourself in check, below is a list of indicators which highlight that you may have distorted the truth.

- *Inflated educational credentials*—For most jobs, there is a minimum educational level and/or a set of qualifications. With these qualifications are associated knowledge and skills. If you do not have the specified qualifications, you should not state that you do. It will look horrible if you enter an interview and are asked questions regarding your degree or what institution you studied at—or worse, if they ask for proof of your qualifications, such as a certificate or your academic transcripts.

- *Omitted or inconsistent periods of employment and/or stretched employment dates*—Gaps in your résumé between one job and another give the impression that you're an unstable employee with little loyalty. If dates overlap or are incoherent in some other way, this indicates that you could be lying about your period of employment. Ensure your dates are correct, and be able to clarify any gaps in your employment.

- *Exaggerated claims of expertise and experience*—Glorifying or upselling your responsibilities and importance in an organisation is a big mistake. You will be unable to elaborate on your involvement on specific projects, the tasks involved, or how you managed multiple tasks with strict deadlines. Be truthful in your answers, as lying can lead to your quick termination if you accept the offer and cannot deliver.

- *Claims of self-employment*— Claims that you were self-employed require verification. This could include an operating website, Australian business number (ABN), business cards, and previous records. If you're unable to produce these documents or forms of proof, you will be considered a liar.

- *Claims of work as a consultant*—The term *consultant* is usually attached to an area of expertise such as "sales consultant" or "HR consultant." If you merely say you were a consultant, the interviewers will expect you to have an area of expertise. They will also ask for previous organisations which have engaged your consultancy services. Do not trap yourself.

- *Vague answers*—Providing vague and general comments under a "responsibilities" section indicates that you might not have been thoroughly involved in your roles. It also can give the impression that you just copied and pasted basic job descriptions from Google or advertisements. If you did have those roles, include points directly from your memory and elaborate on them. Use other job descriptions as a guide to trigger your memory. But remember to avoid being vague!

Good and Poor Résumé Examples

Below are examples of a poor and a good CV. Using the above guidelines, analyse these samples and contrast their differences to determine what makes them good and poor. As an exercise, print off these samples and circle their positive and negative features. Once you've completed this exercise, look at your CV. How does your CV measure up?

A Poor Résumé

14a Barry Street,	Phone: (02) 9676 5050
North Island	Mobile: 0432 397 844
Sydney, NSW 2164	E-mail: lauren.croft@hotmail.com

Lauren Croft

Personal

Name: Lauren Croft

Address: 14a Barry Street
North Island
Sydney, NSW 2164

Telephone: 0432 397 844 (Mobile)
(02) 9676 5050 (Home)

Melissa Hume

Email: lara.croft@hotmail.com

Date of Birth: 6 September, 1994

Education [2007–2012] Year Twelve graduate of
Tomb Raider College, Loon Island

Volunteer and Currently completing Gold Duke of Edinburgh
Co-curricular Scheme
activities Volunteer Sunday School Teacher
Currently plays Soccer for Tomb Raider Underdog
(2005-2012)
Kitchen Helper at Sudanese Integrated Learning
Program
(2011-2012)

School and School Representative for Indoor Soccer (2008)
University Participant in All Schools Cross Country (2008-11)
Participation Solomon Islands Mission Trip (2011)
and Legacy Day (2011)
Contribution 40 hour famine (2009-2012)
Red Cross Shield Appeal (2011)
Walk for Wellbeing (2011)

Skills and Work Concert Band Participant (2007-2010)
Experience Year 12 Year Book Committee (2012)
Year 10 Work Experience at St Vincent's Hospital
(2010)
Australian Business Week (2010)
Defense 2020 Youth Challenge (2011)
RSA Course (2013)
Barista Course (2013)

Referees **Title:** Principal
Name: Mr Hertz Kertz
Phone Number: (02) 8886 6666
Email Address: hertzkertz@wcc.nsw.edu.au

Title: Minister
Name: Costa Coco Coco Senior
Phone Number: (02) 9875 6666
Email Address: macorina.senior@yahoo.com

A Good Résumé

Alexandra Frankie
0408 614 366
alexandra-a-b-frankie@hotmail.com

Career Objective

I am seeking the opportunity to expand my business skills in a new and challenging environment. I would like to acquire a position where I can combine and apply my extensive customer service skills and education. My hard work ethic and enthusiasm have proven to be assets to the organisations in which I have applied myself. My involvement within the property industry has nurtured my time management and communication skills. I hope you will provide me with the opportunity to utilise my skill set and demonstrate my hard work ethic.

Employment History

YOOP CONTACT CENTRE   *2 August, 2010–*
                                     3 August, 2012

Customer Service Officer/Administrator-Expert Team

Responsibilities:

- Customer Service—Inbound/Outbound Calls
- Taking Orders (Sales)
- SAP—Email Enquiries
- Lodge Australia Post Investigations (missing parcels)
- Dealing with customer complaints and enquires
- Corresponding with stores throughout Australia

- Tax Invoices
- Organising replacements of missing products
- Systems Used: SAP (CRM) Emails, Blue Martini, Citrix XanApp—Applications, Data Portal, ECF, MetaFrame (Phone System), website, Microsoft Programs—Excel, Word, Outlook Express

Reason for leaving: Contract position

MIKE BLACKIE PROPERTY SOLUTIONS   *15 November, 2012–current*

Portfolio Manager /Training Specialist

Responsibilities:

- The first point of contact for all staff members regarding training
- Attend to and answer any staff queries with regard to day to day issues
- Manage and service the Private Treaty Team
- Assume greater responsibility and accountability to all LJH PS clients and agents (any issues that arise)
- Work closely with GM on management issues
- Liaise with current and potential clients
- Respond to feedback from the team as to how work is flowing and possible improvements
- Monitor work flows of all staff members on a regular basis to ensure that staff are working at their most effective level
- New staff training
- Audits
- Portal Prioritisation
- Interactive training implementation
- External Portal Training for clients
- Procedure reviews

Achievements: *Promoted three times*

Reason for leaving: Looking for a position closer to home (three hours travel).

REAL ESTATE PORTFOLIOS, NEWCASTLE   *9 May, 2006 –*
                                          30 March, 2007

Sales Associate/Personal Assistant to Angelin Liew

Responsibilities:

- *Leads generator (4–5 listings of my own per month)*
- *Door knocking/Phone canvassing/Letterbox drops*
- *Answering all incoming calls and general queries*
- *Entering property information into Desktop and keeping it up to date*
- *Vendor and/or Tenant Details*
- *Solicitor Details*
- *Property Details, then upload to the appropriate internet sites*
- *Researching past sales RP data (listing presentations)*
- *Open Homes*
- *Private Inspections*
- *Negotiating Offers*
- *Attending to Pest and Building Inspections*
- *Filing, archiving and general office duties*
- *Systems Used: RP Data, Desktop, Microsoft Outlook 2003, Microsoft Word*

Achievements: *Always achieving monthly targets (4 listings per month)*

Reason for leaving: Move away from door knocking

MR LACKEIS REAL ESTATE,   *2 March, 2009 –*
CAMPELLTOWN   *August 2010*

Property Officer

Responsibilities:

- *Open Homes*
- *Letting Properties, Screening prospective Tenants*
- *Condition Reports, Periodic Inspections*
- *Arranging Residential Leases and Signing new Tenancies*

- *Dealing with Landlords, Trades people and Tenants*
- *Chasing Arrears and keeping them to a minimum*
- *Periodic Inspections*
- *Repairs*
- *Leads generator*
- *Systems Used: REST—Evolution—RP Data—TICA*

Achievements: *Always achieving monthly targets*

Reason for leaving: Wanted to expand my knowledge in the property industry.

Qualifications

TAFE HAILBURY College, NSW   *2006–2008*
Certificate IV in Property (Strata Management)

TAFE HAILBURY College, NSW   *2006*
Diploma of Property (Real Estate)

References provided upon request.

Résumé Exercise 1: Writing Achievement Statements

A résumé stand out when it highlights the candidate's unique contributions towards an organisation. It shows that the candidate has gone beyond the confines of his or her job description, exceeded expectations, and hit targets which were not necessarily assigned to him or her or believed to have been within reach. For a potential employer, finding a candidate with major achievements on his or her CV is like finding gold. Achievement statements can make the difference between you being shortlisted or your résumé being tossed to the "okay" pile. How to write effective achievements statements is covered in the following exercise.

Achievement statements must have a situational basis. Briefly outline a specific example from your previous work experience; this involves your skills and knowledge, and highlights the *results* or *outcome* of your contribution.

Each achievement statement must illustrate how your actions were beneficial to your organisation. This can be done without fail by following this simple formula:

Achievement Statement: **Situation** + **Action** → **Results**

Situation: Define your business context and provide a brief outline of your situation.

> *ARSS was a starting up business and required HR policies and procedures to be developed from scratch.*

Action: What action(s) did you take in this situation?

> *I drafted and implemented HR policies and procedures which covered all future employees and was then incorporated using the company's software packages.*

Results: What were the outcomes of your actions?

> *The company was now in the position to manage their employees and create a high standard of compliance for WH&S, code of conduct, and KPI performance, within 1 month of beginning the drafts.*

Create a Summary

A summary incorporates the situation, action, and results into one statement. Providing measurable achievements is recommended.

Example: APSS was placing sole responsibility for event organisation and completion on the fundraising manager. After considering multiple options, I began recruitment and selection activities to find an event coordinator. This saved APSS $1,000 per month, as the coordinator solely designed and implemented a client contact database. This also led to a 60 per cent reduction in event organisation time and fundraising $25,000 in one event—the highest fundraising amount in APSS's history. The fundraising manager has more time to generate corporate sponsorships, leading to the ultimate success of the event.

***Note: After you write an achievement statement, reread it and think, *Is this really an achievement? Would a potential employer read it and think, Who cares?*

Now that you understand what an achievement statement is, it is your turn to practise.

Choose three different situations in which you believed in you solved a problem or exceeded expectations which demonstrate your skills, knowledge, or personality traits. Outline the situation, action, and results of each example. Then ask yourself, *Is this an achievement a future employer would care about?*

Situation 1:

Situation:

Action:

Result:

Achievement Statement:

_____

_____

_____

_____

_____

Situation 2:

Situation:

Action:

Result:

Achievement Statement:

_____

_____

_____

_____

_____

Situation 3:

Situation:

Action:

Result:

Achievement Statement:

_____

_____

_____

_____

_____

Chapter 3

Cover Letters

When you write a cover letter, it needs to be tailored specifically for every job you apply for. Your aim is to prove that you are the right candidate for the role. You need to relate your previous work experience to the job description provided in the advertisement, as the job description tells you exactly what an employer is looking for. Address every point you can, and express your enthusiasm for the role.

Below is a list of action words you can use in your cover letters. They are active verbs; they show initiative and demonstrate that you do not have a laissez-faire attitude toward your work. These are great substitutes for passive verbs.

• Acquired	• Coordinate	• Established
• Adapted	• Corresponded	• Evaluated
• Analysed	• Networked	• Gathered
• Budgeted	• Operated	• Generated
• Built	• Prepared	• Helped
• Calculated	• Program	• Reported
• Categorised	• Promoted	• Represented
• Compiled	Delegated	• Researched
• Completed	• Delivered	• Resolved
• Composed	• Demonstrated	• Reviewed
• Conducted	• Derived	• Simplified
• Constructed	• Developed	• Solved
• Consulted	• Edited	• Succeeded

- Successfully
- Systematised
- Identified
- Implement
- Initiate
- Investigate
- Led

- Maintained
- Make
- Monitored
- Organised
- Produced
- Programmed
- Regulated

- Targeted
- Trained
- Tested
- Utilised
- Verified
- Volunteered

Cover Letter Exercise 1

Your cover letter needs to be written as though this is the only job you have applied for. In your cover letter, put criteria you satisfy from the job description in bold. You've researched the organisation (if it isn't hidden via a recruitment agency), outlined how its mission and values resonate with you as a worker, and incorporated your relevant work experience and major achievements.

Use the cover letter structure template below to analyse the good and poor cover letter samples. Make a comparison and determine how a good cover letter is written. Pay close attention to how the good cover letter example directly addresses the HR administrator job description criteria.

Receiver's Name   Your name
Receiver's Position   Contact number
Organisation   Email
Address

Date:

Dear [receiver's name; if you don't have a name, put "To whom it may concern"]:

Re: Title and reference number of the position for which you're applying.

Paragraph 1: *Position*—demonstrate your enthusiasm towards the advertised position and the organisation. Mention the position type and source of advertisement.

Paragraph 2: *Qualifications*—Address the selection criteria in the job description and how your education has provided you with the necessary skills and knowledge for the position. Use the full name of the degree/certificate, the institution, and the years you began and finished or intend to finish your degree. Highlight your GPA (if it is high), and attach an online version of your academic transcript if it's required or demonstrates competencies in certain subjects.

Paragraph 3: *Employment history, volunteer experiences, relevant extracurricular activities*—You need to demonstrate how your KSAs acquired from your experience are transferable. Elaborate on these experiences, and provide examples where appropriate.

Paragraph 4: *Demonstrate that you have researched the organisation*—Explain how your interest in your role and previous experience ties into your interest in working for the organisation. Show how your values align with the organisation's values. This requires research, but do not quote directly from them. Reiterate what they have stated in your own words.

Paragraph 5: *A thank-you and your availability*—This could be an immediate start, or you may need to provide your current employer two weeks or four weeks' notice. Thank the organisation for their consideration and state that you look forward to hearing from them.

Yours sincerely,

[insert digital signature]

Full Name

Good and Poor Cover Letter Examples

Cover Letter HR Assistant—Bad

Melinda Plume
12a Nightengale Street
Pearlville, NSW 2122
(02) 9894 8264
0401 111 838
Melo.humble@gmail.com
5 July, 2012

To whom it may concern,

I am a confident, polite, hardworking team member able to work effectively while juggling numerous tasks. I'm seeking the opportunity to expand my administration skills and experience in a challenging business environment. I am currently studying a Bachelor of Psychology (Honours) at Macquarie University so that I can pursue this in my future career.

I am applying for the HR assistant position.

I believe I am suitable for this role for the following reasons:

As an administration officer, I have demonstrated strong written and verbal communication skills, experience; ease communicating with a range of people, such as customers, supervisors, managers, area managers. I am also competent with computer programs such Microsoft Outlook, Express, Excel, and using MYOB.

I was highly involved in the recruitment and retention of employees, performance management, WH&S, and developing new policies in my previous position.

The main point of contact was over the phone, and so I have an ease communicating with a range of people. These skills have been reinforced by the completion of the following courses: "Basics of Effective Communication," "Communicating Clearly," and "Working with Difficult People."

My studies currently undertaken at university continue to reinforce the skills necessary in the HR sector of business.

I believe I am an excellent candidate for this role, and I look forward to meeting with you to discuss this position further.

Yours Faithfully,
Melinda Plume

HR Administrator Job Description—Advertisement

HR Administrator, Sydney, APSS (Fictional Organisation)

APSS is seeking an HR administrator to support their HR team.

Primary Purpose

The main purpose of this position is to provide a range of administrative and clerical services to the HR unit in a reliable manner.

Duties

- Prepare all necessary documents for criminal checks, VEVO, working-with-children checks.
- Prepare pre-interview documents and ensure they are properly filled out.
- Conduct reference checks.

- Advise candidates on results of interviews.
- Prepare and issue written offers.
- File and photocopy all documents.
- Respond to incoming queries, and determine what candidates should be assigned to which consultant.
- Manage a busy switchboard.
- Use MYOB to assist payroll on an ad-hoc basis.

Selection Criteria:

- At least two years' experience in administration experience within an HR team.
- Able to assertively provide feedback to unsuccessful candidates.
- Able to maintain confidentiality when liaising with clients and candidates.
- Excellent communication skills—provides timely delivery of information and selects the most appropriate form of communication specific to context.
- Competent in MS Office programs: Word, Excel, PP at an intermediate level.
- Experience with MYOB.

Please apply directly to Alexandra Mitchell via Alexandra. mitchell@onebradley.com.au. For further information, please contact Alexandra on 0401-223-302.

Cover Letter HR Administration Role—Good

ONE Bradley
14 Neckel Drive, Cecil Fields, NSW 2116
0401 111 838
Melo.humble@gmail.com
22 April, 2013

Dear Alexandra Mitchell,

My name is Melissa Plume, and I am currently interested in the administrative assistant role supporting an HR team, advertised by Charterfrank. Studying for a bachelor's in business administration with a bachelor of arts (Psychology) at UTV has nurtured my strong interest in applying my theoretical psychology knowledge, as I have a genuine interest in human resources and project and human development. I believe this position is the opportunity I have been seeking to expand my business experience in a new and challenging environment.

The Recoo All-rounder internship opportunity has created exposure to all aspects of business functioning. Due to my expressed interest in HR and my recruitment background, I've drafted a **HR** manual; documents the process from initial screening of **résumés** to conducting an interview. Other documents include confidentiality and code of conduct agreements. I wrote an advertisement for SEEK to assist in casual selection processes. I have also been highly involved in processing orders and using **MYOB** for invoicing and stock control, entering employee information and timesheet data to organise fortnightly **payroll**. I also file online and sales orders accordingly, follow-up orders with Fastway and assist the team with any other ad-hoc duties. Working closely with the directors, my responsibilities are constantly expanding, and my job has **turned from unpaid to paid recently**. I'm now the HR and payroll assistant.

As administration officer at MELIS Enterprise, I was the first point of **contact face-to-face**, via email, and over the phone **(switchboard)**. I managed a multitude of tasks throughout the day, prioritizing based on urgency and importance. My role involved ensuring consultant and candidate compliance by conducting weekly audits. These audits covered **reference checks**, **VEVO** checks, temp and perm aftercare, and other mandatory documents and assessments. Administration tasks included uploading important applications and test results on the system and utilising Microsoft programs, including **Word and Excel** to process consultant activity, **compliance**, standardise résumés for presentation to clients, and candidate information. I also performed ad-hoc duties as required to provide assistance to the consultants.

My previous role as a sales consultant involved accomplishing **work unsupervised**, prioritizing tasks and ensuring all work was completed. This role also required adhering to strict deadlines with the weekly review and coordination of important team announcements and meetings, **updating the company website,** and ensuring that the administration, technical, and accounting manual were updated monthly. Local dealers and customer bases were regularly contacted according to a schedule and using **data entry** to monitor these interactions.

Effective multitasking was a major component of managing these activities successfully. I also used **MYOB to manage stock inventory levels, send out invoices, and enter payment and customer information. I am still confident with this program.**

If you provide me with the opportunity, I will prove to you that I am hard worker, willing to travel in accordance with the job requirements, and an excellent candidate for this role.

I look forward to discussing this position further.

Yours Sincerely,
Melinda Plume

Cover Letter Exercise 2: Tailoring your cover letter to a Job Description

This exercise has been broken down into three steps.

Step 1: A way to ensure that you address the selection criteria in your cover letter is to use the SEA system.

- S: Skills
- E: Experience
- A: Achievements

When you incorporate SEA into your answer, your answer becomes relevant and concise.

Example

Job description criteria: Successful candidates must be confident using MYOB for stock inventory management and issuing invoices.

Cover letter answer: As a payroll assistant at Vanquish Pty Ltd., I used MYOB to issue invoices, raise purchasing orders, and manage stock inventory levels daily. I also used MYOB to run marginal loss and gain reports on stock, which led to a 15 per cent increase in profits, and I ordered high-demand stock in bulk and reduced low-demand intake.

Step 2: Using a job description you would like to apply for on SEEK, address every JD criteria using SEA system within the confines of your work experience and skills.

Step 3: Once this is completed, take a second look at the good cover letter sample provided above. Does this cover letter use the SEA system? No, but it is still a good cover letter. Now that you have practised using the SEA system, rewrite the HR administrator cover letter according to the retrospective JD.

From this you should notice that you can use the SEA system to transform a good cover letter into a great one.

Now that you understand how effective the SEA system is, apply it to your own cover letters.

Cover Letter Exercise 3

There is always that one job you see advertised and you think, *I have everything but that thing that employer says I must have to be considered.* At this point, you should not forget about the job and keep looking elsewhere. You are still eligible! You just need to turn your void in experience or skill into a positive or an opportunity to learn.

When you're addressing the JD criteria and you come to the point where you do not satisfy it, avoid statements such as "I don't have one year's experience" or "I've never used that software." Turn this gap into an opportunity to demonstrate any other relatable skills and experience. This can include "I can learn MYOB, as for the past two years I have been using a similar software called Xero; this performs invoicing, payroll and stock inventory functions," and "I have over nine months of experience in …"

By using only positive statements in your cover letters, you are selling yourself as a great asset to potential employers, although you might not exactly satisfy their ideal candidate concept.

Now try this with several JDs which you believe you are capable of fulfilling but do not have the desired skills or experience. Write a cover letter for each using SEA and transforming your gaps into an enthusiasm to learn or a way to further build on already acquired skills and experience.

Chapter 4

Interviews

Pre-interview Checklist

Below is a checklist of questions which you should have answers to well before an interview. Being prepared will ease your nerves, improve your interview performance, and leave you feeling as though you did the best you could do.

☐ What time is the interview?

☐ What am I going to wear?

☐ Have I organised my portfolio folder with all my relevant qualifications, references, certificates, transcripts, most recent CV, and a sample from previous projects undertaken?

☐ Have I thoroughly researched the organisation?

☐ What is the organisation's address? Have I printed off a map? Do I know how long it will take to get there, leaving enough time in case I'm lost?

☐ Who will I be meeting with (first and last name, and title within the organisation)?

☐ Have I rehearsed both situation- and behaviour-based questions relevant to the job role?

☐ Have I constructed a list of concise questions to ask the interviewer after the interview?

☐ *Am I ready for the interview?*

Pre-interview Exercises

Exercise 1

Preparation is vital for a successful interview. Below are some exercises you can undertake before an interview to provide you with some structure to your answers and bring important points to the forefront of your mind.

Strengths Exercise

What are your main strengths? What unique strengths can you contribute to this role and the organisation? Why should they select you above all other candidates?

Make a list of the following:

- Technical skills
- Transferable skills, such as communication, leadership, working in a fast-paced environment
- Personality traits, such as tenacity
- Qualifications
- Specific experiences you believe are relevant to the available position

Areas for Improvement Exercise

What are your weaknesses? What actions do you take to improve them?

Make a list(s) of the following, and discuss the action you would take to improve each one; also advise how others would also be able to improve in this area.

- Areas you need to improve in
- Levels of competency
- How you can change your weaknesses into an opportunity to learn

Exercise 2: Demonstrate Your Skills, Knowledge, and Personality Traits to Yourself

This exercise is great for helping you gain an understanding of what type of job you are suitable for, will enjoy, and are skilled and qualified to fulfil. Fill out the table honestly. Print out multiple copies of this sheet and add to it as you continue to learn, change jobs, and acquire more qualifications.

How much do you enjoy it? Scale from 1-10: 1= do not enjoy it at all, 10= highest level of enjoyment. *Beginner, Intermediate, and Advanced* refer to levels of personality trait expressionism, amount of knowledge, and degree of skill competency possessed.

Skills, knowledge, personality traits	Beginner	Intermediate	Advanced	How much you enjoy it

Exercise 3: STAR

From exercise 2, you should have a clear idea about what skills, knowledge, and attributes you have and how they can benefit employers. You must communicate this understanding to employers in an interview. But first, do you know what employers want?

Every employer is different and is seeking different skill sets and personality types according to its job vacancies. Despite this, there are common qualities employers seek:

- Technical skills
- Organisational skills
- Communication skills
- Teamwork skills
- Interpersonal skills
- Strong work ethic
- Ability to handle pressure
- Adherence to strict deadlines
- Attention to detail

When you prepare for an interview, you need to try to demonstrate that you have these qualities. The best way to prepare an answer is to use STAR. The STAR method is fantastic for answering behavioural-based questions.

Behavioural questions are used to elicit information from a candidate with reference to previous behaviour. The theory behind this is that previous behaviour predicts future behaviour. "Provide me with an example of when you had to complete multiple tasks simultaneously and before set deadlines. How did you go about managing these tasks?" is an example of a behavioural question. This question is assessing your ability to handle pressure, to organise, and to prioritise tasks according to their importance.

Using STAR, you can answer the above question.

S: Provide a situation and context.

T: What were the task(s) involved?

A: What action(s) did you take to manage the tasks?

R: What were the results of your actions?

When you use STAR, it is best to provide as many details as possible, with names, dates, figures, and a context. This makes your example more believable. Do not provide false examples, as the interviewer may ask you to elaborate further if he or she suspects you are lying.

When using STAR, use experiences that are most relevant to the job vacancy.

Now it's time for the exercise …

For each desirable quality, create a STAR answer drawing from your experiences. If you have no previous employment history, you can use experiences from studying at university, TAFE, or volunteering.

Technical Skills

S: _____

_____

_____

T: _____

_____

_____

A: _____

_____

_____

R: _____

_____

_____

Organisational Skills

S: _____
_____
_____

T: _____
_____
_____

A: _____
_____
_____

R: _____
_____
_____

Communication Skills

S: _____
_____
_____

T: _____
_____
_____

A: _____
_____
_____

R: _____
_____
_____

Teamwork

S: _____

_____

_____

T: _____

_____

_____

A: _____

_____

_____

R: _____

_____

_____

Interpersonal Skills

S: _____

_____

_____

T: _____

_____

_____

A: _____

_____

_____

R: _____

_____

_____

S: _____

_____

_____

T: _____

_____

_____

A: _____

_____

_____

R: _____

_____

_____

Handling Pressure

S: _____

_____

_____

T: _____

_____

_____

A: _____

_____

_____

R: _____

_____

_____

Adhering to Strict Deadlines

S: _____

_____

_____

T: _____

_____

_____

A: _____

_____

_____

R: _____

_____

_____

Attention to Detail

S: _____

_____

_____

T: _____

_____

_____

A: _____

_____

_____

R: _____

_____

_____

Interview Tips

So you're at the interview stage. This means you've passed the CV screening and the telephone filtering process, and the employer believes you are potentially the right candidate for the position. From this you can extrapolate that you have the desired technical and hard skills required on paper. The interview is your chance to get the job! You need to show them that you can fit into their organisational culture and that you're enthusiastic about the role.

So how do you become the standout candidate? *You prepare.*

Interview preparation reduces the amounts of *ums* and *errs*. It is a fantastic way to make your answers concise. Going into an interview unprepared is one of the worst things any candidate can do.

A great mindset to adopt is that you're a product. You need to market yourself to the potential employer (customer), demonstrating your best features (attributes), the overt benefits (how you benefit their organisation), and why you're the best choice (comparison to other candidates). You cannot do this without preparation!

Presentation

The rule of thumb is always to dress one level above the organisation's standard. For example, if its dress code is smart casual, you dress smart business attire. You can determine the appropriate dress code by calling reception well before the interview. They will likely be happy to inform you and to provide information about the organisation which could be useful during the interview.

Women

- If you are wearing a skirt, make sure it is not too short. Also wear closed-toe in shoes. A jacket over a nice top (not too revealing) gives a professional edge.
- Make sure you are well groomed; if your hair is long, tie it back and keep it away from your face.
- Use natural and light makeup.
- Have clean, natural nails with no bright nail polish.
- Avoid too much jewellery.
- Avoid strong perfume.
- Avoid smoking before the interview, and if that is not an option, bring breath mints.
- Don't forget to smile with your teeth!
- Give a firm handshake.

Men

- Wear a business suit with business shirt and matching tie.
- Make sure you are well-groomed and clean-shaven, and that your haircut is neat.
- Avoid smoking before the interview. If that is not an option, bring breath mints.
- Wear polished business shoes.
- Don't forget to smile with your teeth and give a firm handshake.

Plan Your arrival

Follow the pre-interview checklist. This is the best way to ensure you arrive at least ten minutes early. Punctuality is a strong indicator of professionalism and is necessary if the role involves adhering to strict deadlines.

Switch your mobile phone off! Although you might be kept waiting before the interview, do not use your phone. Read a magazine or a newspaper. Using your phone projects a negative image.

First Impressions

The expression "First impressions matter" rings true, especially in an interview. Humans are visual creatures, so an impression is initially formed by the way you look. This is why presentation is so important. Within the first couple of seconds, you need to project confidence and ensure that their first impression of you is a positive one.

A firm handshake does not mean the tighter the better; you do not want to crush their fingers. You want the palm of your hand to slip into theirs and your thumb and fingers to have a firm grip. While you shake their hand, you should smile—you need to show teeth. Showing teeth is received more positively by the brain than a half or fake smile.

Job Description

Part of your preparation involves knowing what is in the job description. This allows you to demonstrate your skills and knowledge related to the specific role while you're being interviewed. It also allows you to understand what type of information the employer is trying to elicit from you.

Body Language

Be sure to monitor your body language. Most of what you say about yourself does not come from your words but from your body language. Keep your posture straight, do not fidget, and keep your feet flat on the floor. This will keep you grounded. When you explain things, use your hands to emphasise points; open palms are positive body language.

Closing

Prepare some business-focused questions to ask the interviewer. For example,

- What type of management style is used?
- What are the team dynamics?
- How will performance be measured?
- What does the interviewer like about the company?

At the end of the interview, make a *close*: "Is there anything I have or haven't said that would prevent me from entering the next stage in the interview process?"

Thank the interviewer for his or her time and shake hands after the interview.

The first interview is an inappropriate time to ask about pay packages and superannuation, because you haven't been offered the job yet. Never give the client details about your current or previous pay packages, as this could convince them that they can get away with paying you less.

Important Information

Recruitment consultants are essentially like you and me. They have interests and hobbies, likes and dislikes. Do not be afraid of them when you walk into an interview. Be confident. Pretend you're walking into a room and meeting a stranger who is very interested in getting to know all about your work history and your aspirations for the future. *How flattering!*

The Most Popular Interview Questions

Interviewers tend to ask general questions in the first few minutes of the interview. Some of them are icebreakers; others are trying to determine quickly whether you're worthy and are a strong candidate or not.

Below are questions I've encountered in almost every interview. Not all of them will be asked, but it is good to prepare an answer for each one, just in case. I've also included appropriate answers to each question. Use these as a guideline, and personalise your answers to your experience, ambitions, industry, and position type.

Tell me about yourself.

This question is an icebreaker. It gives you time to relax and be at ease. It is an opportunity to have a small chat about who you are. You need to remember that what you say is still being judged. You can say, for example, "I enjoy socialising with friends and playing soccer on the weekend." Elaborate a little, but don't give them a long story about your life. You do not have to include how you enjoy drinking and played with a hangover and still managed to score three consecutive goals. Tell them enough information to give them a sense of who you are, but be careful about the information you include.

It's also a good idea to ask them, "What part of my life would you like me to talk about?" as their question is quite broad. They will most likely opt to focus on what you're like at work. If this is the case, great. You can mention how you enjoy working with people to achieve a common goal or working independently to reach your own targets which challenge you. Provide examples which you believe would relate to the job position.

Here are some words and phrases to avoid when trying to describe yourself:

- *I'm an expert.* This denotes you are a very knowledgeable person with a specific skill set in a particular area. This includes a prolonged and extensive experience involving research and practical application. If this does not accurately reflect your work experience, it is a mistake to state you're an expert during an interview.

- *I'm ambitious.* The interviewer will recognise that you intend to project your driven nature and desire to achieve, so you do not need to say this explicitly. Let your personal presentation and CV demonstrate these qualities, as you do not want to be perceived as too self-absorbed.

- *My performance is outstanding/excellent/exceptional.* These adjectives are perceived differently by people. That is why these words are dangerous. Your interviewers may have high expectations of you, and this could get you into trouble if you're hired and cannot deliver. Let them judge your previous performance. Avoid using words like these.

- *I'm a bubbly individual.* Interviews are designed to test your soft skills rather than your hard skills. Soft skills include aspects of your personality, communication abilities, and personal presentation. If you are naturally bubbly, this will shine through in the interview. Therefore, it is redundant to state in an interview or on your CV.

- *I don't know.* If you're asked to describe yourself and you cannot provide an answer to an icebreaker, the interviewer will think you will be incapable of providing an answer to the following (more difficult) questions. Avoid saying "I don't know" at all costs by practicing mock interviews and preparation.

What do you enjoy most in your current job?

This question is trickier than it appears. The interviewer is trying to see if you can come up with immediate answers and if you're enthusiastic. If you hesitate or your answers are bland, he or she will sense that you do not like it. This can potentially ruin your chances if your current job is quite similar to the position you're applying for. You also don't want to start talking about aspects you do not like. The safe bet is to say that you thoroughly enjoy your current job and it's hard to choose one or two aspects which are your favourites. In saying this, they will question why you're looking for a new job.

If this occurs, you need to mention that this new job is an opportunity that exposes you to aspects you would like to develop further. This opportunity is not provided in your current organisation.

Why do you want to leave your job?

No matter what your real reason is for your job search, what you tell them cannot be a negative reason. You should not mention that your boss is overbearing, you've been turned down for a promotion, or you are bored with your current job. Although your reasons are justified, the interviewer wants to hear only positive answers.

Providing an answer such as "I want to expand my experience in customer service and I feel as though I can best do that in a different organisation," or "This position entails a lot of customer service, and this is an area I would like to further develop my skills." These answers are more appropriate than elaborating on how arrogant your boss is.

What do you think this role involves on a day-to-day basis?

This is one question you must be prepared for. If you seem unsure, the interviewer will wonder why you applied—or worse, if you have applied to every job under the sun? A suggestion is that you can gain an insight into the job roles from looking at the job description or talking to other professionals in a similar industry and/or position. Concentrate particularly on responsibilities. If the job title is similar or is the same as your current job, you can answer this question with reference to your own experience. If there are differences, the interviewer will identify them. This is a great opportunity to be inquisitive. Ask them to explain the differences and mention which differences most interest you.

What do you know about our company?

It is expected that you know what type of products or services the company provides, unless a recruitment consultant is interviewing you. In that case, their client (the organisation) is kept confidential until you're invited to the next interview stage. You should look up the organisation's values and mission statement to gain a sense of their organisational culture. You are not expected to know specific details about products, but look at their news section. If appropriate, mention any new deals the organisation has made. Candidates who demonstrate a knowledge of the organisation are more impressive than those who say, "To be quite honest, I do not know, but perhaps you can tell me."

Why do you want this job?

You need to mention two key points. The first is why you want to work for that particular organisation. The second is why you want this job position. Integrate as much information you know about their company into your answer.

How long would you expect to stay with this company?

Organisations want to know that you plan on staying with them for a minimum of two to three years. Turnover and training new employees cost organisations a lot of time and resources. They want to know that you're worth investing in. It can be challenging to convince potential employers if you constantly change jobs, showing little commitment or loyalty. The only way you can positively justify your frequent job changes is to state "I've been searching for a job within an organisation which challenges me and provides opportunities to develop myself, and in which I want to stay for the long run." They cannot argue with that!

Where do you see yourself in five years?

Another trick question … surprise, surprise! You do not want to be too specific with this question. If you indicate a goal which the organisation cannot fulfil, an X has gone across your name. State broad ambitions and indicate how your goals constantly change, but remember that they want to know that you are driven. A person with no vision is not what an organisation wants. Responses that I highly recommended avoiding when answering this question include but are not limited to the following:

- "I would like to be in his/her position" (pointing to an interviewer who is your senior).
- "I'm seeing where life takes me."
- "I'm not too sure at the moment for five years, but I can tell you in two years …"

How would your colleagues describe you?

If you're going to say you're a team player and you always look forward to helping out your colleagues when possible, make sure this can be backed up by your referees. If you're not the most outgoing person, don't lie because you think that's what the interviewers want to hear. Put a positive spin on it. You can say, "My colleagues will note that I'm not the loudest person, but when it comes to teamwork, I contribute and am always willing to support and assist others when they need help."

Why should we choose you over all other candidates?

I personally hate this question with all my soul. There is no right answer, and it's easy to feel that it is the be-all and end-all of the interview. You can give a positive answer. You can tell them that your character and hard work ethic allow you to overcome challenges and reach set targets. You are determined to prove to them that you're the right person for the job and will fit in their organisation.

Overall, you need to be ready. Listen to the questions you are asked. Be concise and do not include irrelevant or waffly answers. Phrase your answers so that they are applicable to the job.

More questions

Below are some questions you must be prepared to answer, thought they are not as popular as the questions above.

What do you value in an employer in terms of attributes, values, and opportunities?

The interviewer will be analysing your answer in these terms: Can we provide them with what they value? Are there enough internal opportunities to meet their career progression needs? Do they understand what our organisation represents and the activities we are involved in? You want your answer to align with the organisation's mission (goals for the future), their values (sense of responsibility as an organisation to their clients, shareholders, and the surrounding community), and the internal promotion, learning and development, and performance appraisal systems available and implemented in the organisation. Researching the organisation is critical to answering this question well.

What type of management style best suits you? How does it influence your performance?

When you answer this question, you must have in mind what type of leadership style the person who fills the vacant position will be under. If the manager is one of the interviewers, you can gain a sense of her leadership style by the way she interacts with you. Is he facilitative in the way he phrase his answers? Is she black-and-white in asking questions? Does he project an overall friendly persona? You should phrase your question based on how you interpret the manger's management style and honesty. If you work best independently and when you are trusted to complete your tasks, explain this to her. Provide an example. If your honest answer does not align well with her leadership style, then you will experience a great deal of stress if you land the job. This is why providing honest answers in interviews is vital.

Provide me with an example of when you've had a confrontation with a colleague at work. What was the outcome?

This question is testing your conflict-resolution skills. They want to know that you will adhere to their organisation's code of conduct and that you will strive to salvage healthy working relationships despite conflict. An answer like "While remaining calm, I asked my colleague when was a good time to talk about the issue. During this discussion, I listened and gave him the opportunity to voice his perspective with the aim to reach a common ground" demonstrates your level of respect for your colleague and your ability to remain professional regardless of heated emotions. Remember to be specific and to provide context to your example so they can understand why your actions were appropriate and effective.

Tell me about some recent goals you have made. How have you gone about achieving them, and did you exceed them?

These goals can be career based or related to your own personal life. Choose an example which describes a difficult goal. It may have involved many setbacks and required developing new ways of reaching your goal by your chosen deadline. The more detail the better, as you need to justify why this was a difficult goal and the obstacles you overcame.

How do you reward other people's accomplishments?

Leaders are responsible for recognising other team members' achievements and contributions, and for rewarding them and providing appropriate feedback. Your method of offering this reward or feedback provides interviewers insight into who you are. They want to know if you take credit for work which is not yours, if you motivate and encourage others to achieve, and if you are capable of recognising notable achievements.

This question is especially important if you're being interviewed for a leadership position.

What do you feel are the most important characteristics of a leader or a manager?

The way to answer is to choose people you idolise and describe their characteristics, providing reasons as to why these are admirable qualities. Using a model provides interviewers with an image of the type of leader you respect (especially if they know of whom you speak).

Reflect on an experience when you went beyond your set job description and exceeded expectations. What did you do, and what was the result?

A question like this is asking for an achievement statement. Outline a situation when you recognised an opportunity for improvement or innovation. What skills did you utilise? What experiences helped you succeed? What was the difference before and after your efforts? How significant was the achievement for your organisation? Achievement statements are great on your CV and should also be used throughout an interview.

Reflect on a time in your career when you were dissatisfied with your position. What aspect of the job did you dislike the most?

Be careful with this question! You do not want to mention an aspect of your previous job you hated that is part of the job for which you're being interviewed. That is why preparation is not done just for fun; it is so you do not dig your own grave. For this question, choose a part of the job which is specific to the organisation and not present in other jobs. This could include using their own software or database, which was ineffective, slow, or impractical. Whatever you say, be honest and strategic in your response.

Questions to Ask in an Interview

At the end of an interview, the interviewer will ask you, "Do you have any questions?" or "Is there anything else you would like to know about the job role or the organisation?" Use this opportunity! It will help you decide if you really want to work for this person (if he or she would be your superior) or organisation. It also allows you to determine whether there is anything that could potentially hinder your application.

It's a great idea to prepare a couple of questions before the interview so that you do not ask random questions at the end, as this could be destructive. However, do not stick to the set of questions below, as some of them may have been answered already during the interview. If this is the case, ask interviewers personally how they like working there, how long they have stayed, and whether they see themselves staying there for an extended period. How they answer these questions can help you determine whether they themselves enjoy working there.

The following questions would be appropriate to ask at the end of the interview.

If I were to get this role, what would my main aims be for the first three months?

This question forces interviewers to imagine you in the role. By making them visualise you working there, it makes their brain believe subconsciously that this is what they desire. This is an implicit process, and interviewers have no idea it is occurring. By getting them to visualise working with you; you achieving certain targets in intervals up to three months, it can give context to your question. The interviewers will have their own physiological response, whether it is negative or positive, to this visualisation. It is also quite advantageous in the sense that the next time they visualise a person in the role, they will automatically picture you there, since this visualisation has already occurred.

This question is great as it is two-pronged. It makes the interviewers visualise you doing the role and think more in-depth about it. They will provide greater detail about specific responsibilities and tasks if they haven't already done so. The more information the better, as you will be able to assess whether you yourself can fulfil their expectations and the role is what you actually want.

What type of person is successful in your organisation?

First of all, this question shows the interviewers your desire to succeed in this role. This is what they want. They do not want someone who just comes to work, signs in, does only what is required for the money, and then clocks out. They want someone determined to do well and to succeed in their organisation.

Secondly, the question gives you an insight into the type of person they want. If they describe someone who is not you, perhaps you will not be able to live up to their expectations. Another perspective is listening to the "ideal" person they want and aim to be that person if you land the role. Either way, it's good to know now rather than having to work it out later.

What do you most like about working for your organisation?

How the interviewer answers this question is paramount. If they struggle to answer the question or what they say is very vague, it can make you wonder why you would want to work for the organisation. Please note that this question will not work on recruitment consultants, who are outsourced by the organisation and so cannot provide an answer.

What keeps you working here?

This allows your interviewers to open up about what keeps them enthusiastic and motivated.

What career path does someone in this position usually take?

Their answer gives you insight into the opportunities you could expect if you were to accept a job offer.

These questions are mere suggestions. If you come up with questions more relevant to the position, by all means ask them. Just remember not to ask questions which have already been answered in the interview as this will frustrate your interviewer.

Saving Yourself

If you think there is something about your work experience or skill set which is bothering interviewers and is causing them to doubt your suitability to the role, now is the time to address it. These questions need to be said in a way which does not make you appear desperate. You can ask— only if you believe the interviewer would be receptive to this question—*"Is there anything about my work experience you would like me to elaborate on further?"* or *"Is there anything about my CV which is making you doubt my suitability for this role? If so, can we please address it?"*

These questions are very direct and so come with a warning. Some interviewers find this approach very confrontational, so it can lead to a strike-out for you. However, it could save you. The interviewer might respond with a yes and start answering. Phew … you've salvaged the situation and can now walk away knowing you've answered as much as possible to the best of your ability.

How Your Answers Are Judged

HR consultants, future employers, and HR managers do not want you to know the information that follows: how they assess your interview answers. They often use are clearly defined skills set out on the table. Every time you are asked a question, it is linked to one of these skills. How you answer the question is then judged and given a score (usually out of five). After all the questions have been asked and answered, and the scores are added, the candidates with the highest scores progress to the next interview stage.

The scoring description varies between industry, interviewers, and employers. However, the generic rating descriptors are as follows:

- Score 5/5—answer was significantly above what was expected for satisfying the job criteria and forecasting successful job performance
- Score 1/5—answer provided was vague and was well below what was expected and required to fulfil a job description successfully

Rating scales are often used between two interviewers, with their average mark being the final score allocated to each candidate. The same interviewers are used for all rating of candidates to maintain consistency.

Interviewers design questions to test your key skill sets. Key skills can include but are not limited to the following:

- Managing people
- WH&S compliance
- Taking initiative
- Building successful teams
- Leadership and management skills
- Qualifications
- Enthusiasm for the role
- Sales ability and persuasiveness
- Display of ethics
- Working independently
- Teamwork
- Prioritizing tasks according to importance
- Organisational fit

Evaluation matrixes can also include the following factors:

- *Handshake*—Did the candidate greet the interviewer with a firm handshake for an appropriate amount of time? Was the handshake accompanied by a smile? Did he have strong eye contact?
- *Greeting and personal introduction*—Did the candidate greet the interviewer using their name? Did she demonstrate an approachable demeanour?
- *Appearance*—Did the candidate present professionally, wearing a business suit, natural makeup (female), hair appropriately groomed, shoes polished, clothing suitable for the organisational culture?
- *Level of interview preparation*—Did their answers demonstrate that they had researched the organisation, and did they have appropriate materials for the interview, including a copy of their updated résumé?
- *Use of eye contact*—Eye contact was direct and did not make the interviewers feel uncomfortable.

- *Language and tone*—The candidate used appropriate grammar, volume, vocabulary, and rate of speech, and spoke without mumbling.
- *Body language*—The gestures used were appropriate to emphasise the points made. Posture, seated and standing, was good and was not hunched or slouched.
- *Questions asked of the interviewer*—Questions asked were used to gather greater insight into the organisation, the interviewer's own experiences within the organisation, and knowledge sourcing about job expectations. Questions asked demonstrated prior interview preparation. Responses to questions were noted.
- *Enthusiasm for the position*—Enquired when she would find out about the selection decision. Candidate reaffirmed her interest in the position to the interviewer. She asked for the job and highlighted her suitability for the role.
- *Interview closure*—The candidate was appreciative of the interviewer's time and consideration for the position. He initiated a handshake, maintained eye contact, smiled, and was thankful?

Now that you know the extent to which you could be judged before, during, and after an interview, you can ace it! Use the insight provided in this chapter to stay on par with your interviewer(s) and land your number-one job.

What to Include in Your Interview Folder

It's important to have an interview folder because

- it reminds you of what you've done;
- it instils confidence; and
- it makes you seem more prepared.

The purpose of your interview folder is to help sell yourself in ways you can't during the interview. It provides proof of your skills and abilities through certifications, achievements, and contributions to your industry. What's included is reliant to the industry or job you're applying to.

1. Creating a portfolio is great interview preparation. It reminds you of all your previous work experience, how you have an opportunity to organise it into a coherent order. You also begin to articulate your work experience, which will assist your communication during the interview.

2. What you include must be relevant to the job you're applying for. You do not have to include every certificate or sample of work you have ever done. You should include the most relevant, the most outstanding, and what best demonstrates your suitability to the role. For example, if you are applying for a role in an RSL, the RCG certificate would be appropriate. However, if you're applying for an administration role, you do not have to include this in your folder.

3. The folder you use should look new; the plastic sleeves should not be crinkled. Original certificates should be used. Laminating your certificates will protect them and give the impression that you take pride in your achievements.

Passing Assessment Centres

Assessment centres are a difficult and complex form of recruitment and selection. Multiple stages are involved; these are used by corporate organisations to discern positions of importance and where they require the right candidate. Passing these assessment centres requires tenacity, preparation, and a desire to beat those whom you're competing against. I will share my own personal experience on passing each stage. From my experience, you will begin to understand the processes involved and the steps needed to pass.

In October 2013, I applied for an HR coordinator role for company A. I was informed of this opportunity via email, as they worked in conjunction with Company B's program to select their annual intakes. The email was as follows:

Dear Student:

Company A is once again offering university [number] students the opportunity to apply for its X Program for 2014. Students who are selected for this program will gain hands-on experience working full time for Company A while studying and being paid a scholarship through Company B. This is a wonderful opportunity to start your career while still at university.

Company A is looking for students interested in marketing and human resources positions. There are X positions available through the X Program.

To find out more about the positions and to apply, please click on the link below.

Please Note:

Students who wish to apply must have completed their second year of study and be able to enrol in X and X in 2014 as part of their program of study

All positions are located at X.

Successful students must be available to start their placement in [date].

Applications close on [date].

The job description was attached with links to their website and appropriate information. I immediately updated my CV and highlighted the aspects of my role at the time, outlined in the job description. I also wrote a tailored cover letter linking aspects of HR I'd initiated and contributed to my current organisation and how these skills could be further developed through Company A's learning and development program.

Once I had submitted my application, there was that ever-so-pleasant wait for a phone call. Within a week of my submission, a recruitment associate to arrange a telephone interview called me. He advised that I would need to elaborate on my previous work experience and the reasons I wanted a role at Company A. With this I knew I'd need a background knowledge of the company, the corporate social responsibility activities they were involved in, and how I could convince them that I really wanted the role. I scheduled a time when I would be in a quiet environment, with few interruptions, and where I was comfortable.

Once I had received the confirmation for the telephone interview, I prepared and wrote brief notes on the job description. I had this in my hand while I was being interviewed. The telephone interview lasted about fifteen minutes. While I was being questioned, I could hear the interviewer frantically hitting his keyboard, trying to capture as much detail as possible. I tried to slow down a little and to make my answers more concise. Once he had finished the interview, I asked when I would know if I had progressed to the next stage. He said about a week, and that was the end of it.

About a week later, I received a phone call telling me I was invited to an assessment day on Company B's premises. They stated the date and asked if I was available. I said I was. They informed me they would send a confirmation email. I had never undergone an assessment process; I had only read about it. I was enthused that even if I didn't end up with the role, it had been a great learning experience.

Two days after that call, I noted that I still had not received the confirmation email. With only a first name and a Melbourne number, I called and tried to find out who was responsible for sending the confirmation email. Eventually I got through, and they apologised for the delay. That afternoon an email was sitting in my inbox. I thought this could have been either an honest mistake or a way of weeding out those who were sincerely interested. Either way, the follow-up call was needed.

Below is a copy of the confirmation email:

Hi there,

Congratulations on being selected to attend the Company A Assessment Day. As per our discussion, please find below the details for the day.

Date: *Thursday, _____2013*

Time: *8.30am–3pm at the latest*

Address: *Company B's main foyer: Level 1, Room 2A*

What to bring with you: *Please bring an original copy and a photocopy of your transcripts.*

Dress: *Smart business attire*

Activities on the day: *After a short introduction and brief overview of the program and Company A, you will be assessed by a team of managers and recruitment consultants during various activities which include a group presentation, an individual and a group exercise, and a 30-minute behavioural interview.*

Presentation: *Please prepare a 5-minute presentation on a hobby or something you are passionate about. You will be presenting in front of some of the hiring managers and other students. Please note you will not be required to use any technology during your presentation.*

If you have any further questions regarding your interview or there is a need to reschedule your appointment, please do not hesitate to contact me on the details below.

As you can see from the email, preparation was needed. A five-minute presentation was required, and the subject matter was broad. I didn't have any issue with public speaking or talking without notes, but this threw me.

I was stuck. I wasn't about to tell them what I was passionate about, which was running my own business, as this counteracted what I would want out of the program. And my hobbies weren't that interesting, in my opinion. The only thing I knew I could talk about that would be interesting and different from what other people could offer was my life as an identical twin. So that's exactly what I did. I didn't prepare a scripted speech or draft palm cards. I brainstormed ideas which would be appropriate to potential employers.

I divided my presentation structure into three segments: the positives and negatives of being an identical twin, some funny and unique stories, and a discussion of the unique sense of responsibility I got from it. This included my participation in twin studies for research.

I thought a nice icebreaker would be a good way to start me off. I printed a picture of me and Amy (my twin) standing side by side with the letter A and B under the pictures. I planned to ask the audience which they thought was me in the picture. I figured people would like this, since they'd enjoyed it throughout my life. That was the extent of my preparation.

A couple of days before the appointment, I printed off a copy of my academic transcripts. I also worked out what time I had to catch the bus and what I would be comfortable wearing, as it was going to be hot.

Interview day came, and I was ten minutes early, as planned.

I entered the room, said hello to the organiser, and got my name tag. I started talking to people I had never met. I asked them what role they were applying for and what degree they studied at university. Eventually the room started filling up, and the induction began. They briefed us about Company A and presented 2012's program experiences and what we could expect to gain from the program. We were then given the day's schedule, and off we went for presentation time.

Due to a lack of time, the presentation time allowed was reduced from five minutes to three. The panic was obvious on candidates' faces. People had palm cards and prepared speeches. It would be difficult for them to adapt their speech with two minutes cut out. I believe this was part of the test to see who panicked when circumstances changed and who could be flexible. I welcomed the opportunity and volunteered to present first. Others also volunteered, and I was third.

While watching the first two speeches, I noted what they did that made me drift off and what kept me listening. I noticed that none of them moved; they didn't use their hands, and they didn't engage their audience with their eyes.

Then it was my turn. I got up and said my full name and what role I was going for. I cued to the timer, and off I went. People were enthused at trying to tell Amy and me apart, but I only gave them thirty seconds. My storytelling involved movements, hand gestures, and changes in the volume of my voice to emphasise a point. It all lasted three minutes and ten seconds. I sat down and relaxed.

The next stage was the one-on-one interview. I was assigned Mary and Maxine. The interview room was on the opposite side of campus, and I was leading them. Because we were behind schedule, we began talking about my experiences along the way. This was a casual conversation. Finally, when we got to the room, they asked me behavioural questions which I needed to relate to my previous experience. I was also given the opportunity to ask any questions that I had. And then it was time for lunch.

After talking to the different graduates while eating, I had to do an individual task. This assessed my ability to manage different tasks with deadlines and to prioritise according to their importance. I was provided half an hour to complete the task. Before rushing into it, I breathed in, read through the document three times, and gathered what they were actually trying to assess. There are no right or wrong answers. Company A recruitment associates were assessing my thought processes how I was able to justify the order I put each task in and how I recognised their level of importance. After this, the task wasn't a difficult one. I just made sure every order assigned was justified.

The group task came. I knew that one person who was particularly overbearing would try to control of the task and assume a leadership position. He had been overbearing all day, and I knew I couldn't allow him to tell me what to do. I also had to be cooperative, to contribute my own ideas towards the assigned task, and to work with the team. I had to do all this while being watched by a team of recruitment associates. This would be the decider.

There were six participants: two young women, including me, and four young men. We were seated at a table and handed clues to solve the problem. We were not allowed to exchange clues or put them down. We had to communicate verbally. The problem was that there were five different-coloured houses. Each owner of each house was of a different nationality and had a particular pet as well as a drink and a fruit they liked. We had to work out who had the fish.

We began sorting through the order by standing up, with our bodies representing the houses. With six participants, I named myself the landlord against the overbearing person's instructions, and I helped the other team members organise themselves. I listened and then advised them on what to do next. I was putting in ideas without dismissing others' contributions. Eventually our thirty minutes was up, and we had solved the problem. The day was finally over.

I handed over my academic transcripts and said goodbye to some of the assessors I had worked with closely.

Although this was a long-winded story, you can learn something from it. To pass through the stages, you must believe in your own ability, think on your feet, and be yourself. The process is difficult and intense at times. Surviving the day is an accomplishment in itself. If you ever have to undergo an assessment centre process, remember that each stage is unique to the role(s) offered and to the organisation. Be prepared and confident in yourself. That is how you will succeed.

Giving the Right Impression

From the moment you walk into an organisation, your interview has started. Everyone is watching how you behave and interact with the people in the foyer, and the receptionist is watching as you make your presence known. You need to keep this in mind, as you do not know who has been incorporated into the recruitment process.

When I went for an interview for a multibillion-dollar organisation, I was unaware of the complexity of the recruitment process. Although it had taken two months to progress to the face-to-face interview stage, the recruitment process started with the initial application, a telephone interview, and an online aptitude test.

I remember entering the level-eighteen foyer, smiling, and being friendly to the receptionist, letting her know that I'd arrived for my ten o'clock appointment. She noted that I was early and asked me to sign off. She gave me a tag stating my full name and the time I had arrived. She then offered me a seat where there were two lounges perpendicular to each other in the middle of the foyer, with a singular chair opposite them. Before sitting down, I politely asked the receptionist if there were any cafés or places to eat lunch close by. This started a conversation which led to discussing the amazing view and how much she enjoyed looking at it every day at work.

Eventually I took my seat and started talking to a gentleman named Arthur to my right on the second couch. I smiled at the man sitting in the single chair, but he was engrossed in his iPad. My conversation with Arthur lasted fifteen minutes as we waited. I discovered he too was waiting for an interview, but for a different position; he told me how this position related directly to his studies. He was called up first, and I wished him all the best for his interview.

Five minutes later I was called into a meeting room with the organisation's recruitment consultant. The interview went well but was cut short by a practise evacuation procedure. I left on a positive note and was contacted two weeks later for another face-to-face interview in the next stage of selection. This was not due to my performance in the short interview, but due to my interaction with everyone from the moment I'd walked into the foyer. The man in the single chair had been taking notes on my interaction with the other candidate. He noted my genuine and sincere nature and my ability to communicate with a range of people.

In order to be successful, you need to show the employer who you really are. You also need to be aware that some steps in the recruitment process are not obvious. You must keep this in mind.

Another thing you should note is that receptionists act as gatekeepers. As the first point of contact for the organisation, they possess an abundance of information. You should ask them whether they enjoy working at the organisation and how long they have worked there. It is best to pay attention not to what they say, but to how they say it. Being in their work environment, they are less likely to be honest if they are not happy. If what they are saying contradicts what they really feel, it will be apparent through their body language, tone, and enthusiasm when they talk about their current employer.

Receptionists can also be involved in the recruitment process. In large recruitment agencies, the administration officers are the first people to meet and greet candidates. They try put them at ease and take them to an interview room. Before the interview, the consultants ask the administration officer what the candidates were like—if they were anxious or calm, and their degree of presentation. These comments matter in their impression formation and can at times be a determining factor in whether they send you through to meet with their client (the employer) or you are not put forward for consideration.

Based on my own personal experiences, I constructed the table below with information on how you can make a positive impression in the minds of those who matter.

What to do

- Be friendly and polite to everyone you come into contact with.
- Be approachable, smile when it's appropriate, and be friendly.
- Always address the receptionist politely.
- Wait patiently for your interview. Don't complain, and make sure you're not looking too much at your watch. Your phone should be out of sight, switched off or on silent. Do not use your phone to look at the time.
- When you're waiting, sit up straight. Do not slouch, and avoid yawning if you can.
- Read the information provided in the waiting area. Usually it contains useful information about the organisation. You can use this information in the interview, which can make you appear that you have done your researched and are up-to-date on what's been happening within the company.
- Give a firm handshake. A lot of people believe that this indicates whether a person is confident, competent, and capable of fulfilling the job.
- Maintain positive body language.

What not to do

- Avoid indulging your nervous habits. Make an active effort not to fidget, play with your hair, etc.
- Maintaining eye contact when spoken too is important. But do not stare. Do not avoid eye contact.
- Avoid negative body language, such as folding your arms or clenching your fists.
- Do not play on your phone or listen to music. You need to wait patiently.
- Always be truthful in your answers. The truth always comes out, especially when you have multiple interviews and your answers begin to appear inconsistent.

My Experience as a Recruitment Officer

As an administration officer at a recruitment agency, I served as the bridge between the candidate and the recruitment consultant. I interacted constantly with both sides, so I grew to understand their individual perspectives. From this experience I learnt a lot about myself, how unemployment affects candidates in unique circumstances, and various ways others can help them. I also learnt how tough the recruitment arena can be, despite Australian legislation promoting equal employment opportunities.

From my personal experiences, I hope to enlighten you on how recruitment agencies and corporations operate. You will see how challenging it is to filter through candidates and how easy it is to treat them as numbers rather than persons. I also hope to give you insight into the methods you can use to improve your chances of success if you must go through a recruitment agency to find your next job.

Please remember that recruitment agencies provide a service and have their place in society. Companies choose agencies to outsource their recruitment and selection activities, as they are professionals and experts in this field. Recruitment consultants can be quite helpful in finding a job and securing your future for yourself and your family.

I'd like to start with my own recruitment experience. I saw an advertised position on SEEK for an administration officer supporting a small HR team. I thought this would be great to build upon my brief experience as a recruitment consultant internship, so I applied. The next morning, my I was awakened at 8:15 a.m. by an English-accented woman called Alice. She asked me, "Is now a good time to speak?" I asked her if she could please hold on for one moment. In a few seconds, I scrambled from bed and went over to the printout of the job positions I had on my desk. Now awake, I began answering her questions.

She was intrigued by my answers and noted that my CV looked unstable. I agreed but persuaded her that the reason for changing jobs frequently was that I was exploring what industries and positions interested me. I emphasised that I found human resources and recruitment practises very interesting. She was apparently satisfied with this answer, because I landed an interview.

Just as I walked into their office, I heard a distant buzzing sound, and I didn't know what this was until I was employed. I went over to the desk and looked at their business cards. I took Alice's card and placed it in my pocket. There was a small bell with a sign above it reading, "Please press bell for assistance." Before I could, I was greeted by the administration officer (Doris). She knew I was there to see Alice, and she took me to a meeting room. She explained some of the forms I had to fill out, and we engaged in a brief discussion about how I had gotten lost on the way there.

Once Doris was gone, I was left waiting for five minutes. It was a small room with one wall painted dark blue and a small plaque indicating organisational values. I wasn't nervous, but I was interested to see how the interview would turn out. My boss at my brief recruitment internship had told me about this agency. He insinuated that their practises were poor, that they spent the majority of their time devoted to business development calls rather than focusing on placing candidates and communicating with their clients. This had definitely skewed my perception; I was expecting incompetence. But my boss and I were wrong.

As Alice entered the room, I stood up and shook her hand. We then went through my CV, and she clearly said in her accent, "You're a strange candidate." I think she meant this as a compliment. She was quite professional in her manner and personal presentation. Her questions were concise and open-ended, allowing me to elaborate on my answers.

I left the interview feeling anxious. I had talked a lot and provided in-depth answers, and I was replaying the interview over and over again in my head. The memory of face-palming myself makes me laugh now as I look back. But the memory of being interviewed didn't torture me for long. Later that afternoon Alice invited me to attend a second interview with other members of her team.

Long story short, I landed the job. The message you can take from this story is that it is hard to know if you have performed well or poorly in an interview. The lines are blurred. All you can do is prepare for it, be honest, and sell yourself as best as you can.

Chapter 5

Recruitment Agencies

One of the most important ingredients in any organisation is attracting and retaining high-quality candidates. By *high-quality* I mean individuals who possess the characteristics required by the hiring organisation.

Some large corporations utilise internal HR systems for recruitment and selection processes. However, large organisations often outsource their recruitment activities to agencies. For out-sourced recruitment agencies to fulfil this function, they undergo certain processes. These are outlined in great detail below. Generating an in-depth understanding of how recruitment agencies work can help you to be more prepared for interviews and aware of client and recruitment consultant expectations, thereby increasing your chances of being placed.

The Steps Recruitment Agencies Take

1. Screening of Résumés Specific to Client Needs

The job market at the moment is incredibly tight, and the level of education and expertise expected of a candidate to fill basic roles is increasing. With SEEK advertisements being bombarded with applicants, only those applicants who specifically address the client's needs will be shortlisted and then contacted. Therefore, becoming a competitive and standout candidate is fundamental.

You must effectively sell yourself through your résumé, which requires having a CV. Your CV must market your skills, experience, and qualifications in a positive light. It also must specifically address the criteria outlined in the job advertisement. A lot of job advertisements on SEEK state, "Please note: Only suitable candidates will be contacted."

When recruitment consultants initiate contact, they conduct themselves in the following order:

- Inform you of their name, position, the agency they represent, and the job title to which you've applied
- Ask if it is an appropriate time to speak and if you have at least five minutes to discuss your interest in the position, previous work experience, and future aspirations
- State that they are in the process of shortlisting candidates and will be in contact with you shortly—or arrange an interview time if they were satisfied by your responses over the phone

If an interview is secured, the recruitment consultant will send out an email confirming an interview time, location, and any required documents, such as a visa, reference details, and/or certificates. You will need to respond to the email confirming your attendance. You might receive something like this:

Hi Monica,

Your interview is confirmed for:

Date and Time: Monday 8 July, 2012 @ 3pm

Address: Lvl 1, Suite 4.22, 18 Mexico Drive, Homeland

Parking: Free parking available outside building entrance.

If you can't attend your interview for any reason please contact me on 0411-122-123.

Kind Regards,
Josie Harem

2. Interview

For information on how to conduct yourself before and during an interview, refer to Interviews, Chapter 4.

3. Testing

After the interview, the recruitment consultants may want to you to undergo tests at their office or in the convenience of your own home. Following is an email example sent regarding Microsoft Office testing:

> *Hi,*
>
> *Please complete the following test(s) on your own and without anyone else. Falsification of your preemployment application, including test(s) may be grounds for your application to be dismissed. Falsification includes, but is not subject to having someone else complete the test(s) on your own behalf, having someone assist you with the test(s), and using unauthorised resources.*
>
> *By commencing this test, I acknowledge and agree to the above statement,*
>
> *You have been issued the following eTicket for the MS Office Test.*
>
> *You have X days to complete this test.*
>
> *Please click on the included links to begin. Follow the instructions provided.*

4. Reference Checks

Before recruitment consultants are confident and willing to present you to their client, they first conduct reference checks. Some recruitment agencies require two reference checks from two previous employers within the last two years. Character references can also be taken, but these are less favourable, as they do not provide insight into employee behaviour.

Recruitment agencies must also advise the candidates that they will be conducting these checks and gain permission. In accordance with privacy policy, any information gathered can be accessible by the referee and the candidate.

Once you provide the agency with your referee details, it is not only polite but also conducive to your application to advise them that they will be contacted. Remember to thank your referees before and after for taking the time to answer the consultant's questions, as these can be quite extensive. We also recommend informing them of your application status and if their efforts helped you secure a job. Remember, maintaining relationships is key to a successful career!

An example of a reference checklist:

Reference Check

Candidate: Date Taken:

Referee:

Company:

1) What was their job role?
2) What were the main duties and responsibilities?
3) Were there any areas he or she performed exceptionally well?
4) What would be an area of improvement?
5) Why did he or she leave your company?
6) Was he or he willing to work in teams? Did he or she require constant supervision?
7) What was his or her working attitude? Positive, proactive, lazy?
8) Would you employ him/her again?

5. Client Interview

Before the client interview, they will prep you with a phone call and an email. The email will provide interview tips, instructions on researching the company, and information on what type of presentation is acceptable.

If you're a smoker, avoid having a cigarette before the interview. Any scent of smoke can be a deal breaker, as potential employers associate smoking with taking more breaks during working hours and needing more sick leave.

The email can also take the following form:

> *Hi _____,*
>
> *Thank you for your time earlier on the phone. As discussed please see details of your scheduled interview below:*
>
> **Client:**
>
> **Contact:**
>
> **Date:**
>
> **Location:**
>
> **Website:**
>
> *On arrival please say that you're here for an interview with [contact name].*
>
> *I have attached in this email some advice for preparing for an interview as well as a job description for this role.*
>
> *I will contact you shortly after the interview for some feedback.*
>
> *All the best.*

Provide feedback to the recruitment consultant. Meanwhile, they will contact the client to get their feedback about you.

If your initial interview with the client contact was successful, the recruitment consultant will inform you of the next step. This usually involves meeting with the managing director or another client contact in a higher position to determine whether you are the best fit for the job and the organisational culture.

6. Job Success

If you have reached this stage, congratulations! You have landed the job of your choice.

Now that you have a job, you need to keep it. Below are a couple of tips to impress your new employer as they form their opinion of you and of the type of worker you are. This happens within the first few days of your employment.

On your first day, arrive to work between ten and fifteen minutes early. Greet your employer and introduce yourself to your colleagues and other staff members. Be enthusiastic and eager to learn. Observe the organisational behaviour. Note the levels of presentation, your colleagues' attitude towards their boss, how lunchtime is structured, and the degree of socialisation during working hours—for example, is small talk while work acceptable, or is silence expected?

In your first week, you will not be expected to know everything. You will be allowed to make mistakes. Take this as an opportunity to ask as many questions as possible to minimise your mistakes and absorb as much information as possible. Once your probation period or training is over, this leniency will no longer exist.

Note: Although you might realise that your new job is different from what you expected, you need to remember the competitive and complex process you endured to secure your position. With a tight market, it is not wise to quit a job immediately or while in your probation period. This tarnishes your CV and your reputation as an employee. Also, there is no guarantee that you will secure another job immediately or any time in the near future.

How Recruitment Agencies Make Money

Recruitment agencies provide a brokerage service between their clients and the candidate they are trying to contract. For providing these services, the agencies charge fees either based on a candidate's first annual salary, or these fees are charged only once they successfully place a candidate.

There are two different types of recruiters: retained and contingency.

Retained Recruiters

These consultants generate their total fee as a percentage of the placed candidate's first annual salary. This is usually between 15 to 25 per cent. They receive their payment over the course of three stages:

1. A retainer is an upfront fee charged by the recruiter for initiating services. This retainer is non-refundable and is a small percentage of the total fee. Charging a retainer means an agreement has been made between the client and the recruitment agency; the client will exclusively use one recruitment agency (the one charging the retainer) to fill the job vacancy.

2. Another fee is than charged once consultants have begun shortlisting candidates. This is larger than the retainer and is also a predetermined percentage of the candidate's first annual salary.

3. Once the client has chosen one of the candidates presented by them from the consultant, the remainder of the total fee is paid.

The amount of fees that can reimbursed if a candidate is terminated decreases on a sliding scale over the first three months of placement. After three months, the client cannot be refunded any of the paid fees.

This ensures that recruitment consultants are presenting high-quality candidates, as incompetency will lead to less commission.

Contingency Recruiters

These recruiters take a greater risk. They do not enter an exclusive agreement with the client, and they receive a payment only once they have made a candidate placement. This means clients can engage other agencies' services, and it is a competition amongst these agencies to find the best candidate first. If an agency's candidate is not chosen, the agency receives no payment.

Candidates often wonder if recruitment fees decrease their salaries. Fees remain independent of salaries and are used only to calculate how much is to be charged by an agency.

Recruitment Summary

There are thousands of boutique recruitment agencies in Sydney alone. You can tell the difference between those that are newly established (some are still operating from their apartments) and those that have been around for a while. Established agencies never use the excuse that their office is too busy so they do not have space to book an interview with you. They also do not opt for Skype interviews under the pretence that it is for your convenience.

If you find yourself engaging with a new agency, do not treat that as a negative. Welcome this piece of information, knowing that it is less difficult to secure a further interview with the client.

HR and Recruitment Lingo

Organisations often outsource their HR and recruitment activities to external agencies. This directly affects the candidates. In saying this, having an understanding of what these activities are and mean is extremely useful.

- *Graduate recruitment*—These are the interviewing and selection processes for university graduates on behalf of large organisations.
- *Headhunting*—A recruiter confidentially approaches highly skilled and experienced candidates who already have a job and may not be looking for a job. Consultants represent their client by providing job information.
- *Job descriptions*—In Australia, it is a legal requirement to have a job description for every employee. This is usually attached to the letter of offer. Writing specific and measurable outcomes is important, as ambiguous KPIs and targets do not protect organisations from litigation.
- *Phone and email screening*—Consultants use predetermined structured questions to filter through good- and poor-quality candidates at the early stages of the recruitment process.
- *HR start-up advisory services*—Consultants set up systems, policies, and procedures for an organisation's HR division. These services range from very basic, such as creating WH&S practises, to establishing ISO standards.
- *Shortlisting applicants*—This is a filtering process in which consultants narrow down a list of candidates through emails and phone screening. The candidates which are shortlisted are chosen for the interview stage.
- *Psychometric profiling*—This is conducted by trained organisational psychologists for senior and executive positions. For lower-end positions, psychometric-profiling software can be purchased and administered by consultants electronically to candidates which progress from the interview stage. This profiling often assesses candidates' preferred management styles, motivations, and personality dimensions as well as how they interact with other team members.
- *Induction and training packages*—Consultants develop induction packages for new employees; these follow legislative requirements. They also include information on the organisation and help employees assimilate into their new work culture and job role.

Chapter 6

Additional Help

The reasons people purchase RCI Success's Candidate Program vary widely. They could be currently employed and searching for a change of direction, or seeking to enter the workforce for the first time or after a long absence. Regardless of the reason, it is useful to know what is and is not appropriate to tell your employer.

Things to Never Say and Do in Your Workplace

No matter what work environment you're in, there are a few standard things you should not say to your boss, regardless of the circumstances. The statements below do not have to be spoken, but are messages sent to your employer through your actions, body language, overall attitude, and approach to working individually and in a team. Avoid communicating these messages, as they are likely to increase your chance of termination.

Be unenthusiastic—Although fundamentally everyone works to be paid and earn a living, you do not want your boss to think that is all you're there for. He wants to feel that you believe your work is important and has some value and that you sincerely enjoy the work you do. If you do not, you need to make him believe so. You need to continuously monitor your attitude towards work and remember that a lack of enthusiasm projects that you just want to do what is required and walk away with a payslip. This is not an endearing qualities that will earn you a pay rise, promotion, or career opportunities, so be careful. Monitor your behaviour and your feelings, and if you are just working for the money, perhaps you should consider changing jobs. Jobs which do not satisfy your nonmonetary goals can be harmful to your mental and physical well-being.

Say "That's not my job"—When you join a new organisation, you are given a job description which includes any KPIs, duties, responsibilities, and measures of productivity you need to reach. Organisations and bosses generally expect you to be able to go beyond the confines of your job description without resistance when your team or division requires it. When you complain or say, "That's not my job," you immediately give the impression that you're not a team player. It also shows that you're not willing to put in extra effort to help your organisation reach its targets.

Say "You never told me to do that"—When your boss calls you into her office for a one-on-one conversation and begins to explain about a particular project or job task which has been neglected, your response cannot be "You never told me to do that." If appropriate, take ownership of the work and explain that you were not aware that the task existed or had a particular deadline. Apologise for the miscommunication, and affirm that you will get to work on it straight away. Be tactful with your delivery of this message. Not taking ownership of work outlined in your job description or assigned to you is a big cross against your name.

Point out problems while not looking for solutions—Have you ever felt frustrated when you're in a team and you're trying to solve a difficult problem, and there is one person who identifies the problem but contributes no possible solutions? Do not be a problem spotter. Be proactive in your approach to solving problems. Yes, the first step to solving a problem is identifying that one exists, but do not stop at step one. Think and communicate your ideas to your colleagues and superiors. This is one way to show that you're contributing, taking initiative, and having an active role as a problem solver.

Show no interest in training and new projects—If you are given the opportunity to expand your skill set with additional training or challenging work, show your boss that you're enthusiastic and welcome the challenge. Rejecting the new project or responsibilities is a sure sign that you do not care about your career, and it gives them a cause to doubt your worth in their organisation.

Don't cooperate with changes—A lot of organisations undergo dramatic transformations and restructuring due to prolific growth or downsizing. For these changes to be successful, organisations require the full cooperation of employees. Being the person who points out that changes will take a lot of time and effort is redundant and does not motivate or improve the situation. Be the person who recognises the amount of work required and who derives satisfaction from seeing the end result.

Just ignore a bad situation—If you often think that you could be doing better things with your time, also think of ways to improve your situation. Approach your superiors and suggest systems which could improve productivity or ways your skills could be put to better use. Sitting there dreading your job will be noticed by those around you—and most certainly your boss. So take action to rectify the situation, whether that means fixing your current job or finding a new one.

Let fear of failure stop you—When faced with a new challenge, see it as an opportunity to showcase your competencies and how much you are an asset to your organisation. Although you can become swarmed with fears of failure and inadequacy, you must overcome them. Not finishing your work with the excuse "It was too difficult" communicates incompetence.

Do only what you think you have to—Especially in start-up and small businesses, it is in an organisation's culture that you need to go beyond your normal scope of work to get the job done. People who are unwilling to put in overtime or help other team members manage their workload are seen as unhelpful and selfish. The mindset of clocking in and doing only your set tasks and then clocking out is dangerous. People who adopt it are viewed as only working for the money.

Writing a Professional Email

Whether you're applying for a job in response to an advertised vacancy or reaching out to an employer for which you would like to work for, you need to be able to write a professional email.

Constructing a professional email requires effort and practise. A junior is not expected to be able to write an email which is concise, projects the correct intentions of the responder to the recipient, and generates a positive response. Below is a template to help you fast-track your ability to write good emails. They must be adapted to each message and the context in which each message is framed.

Subject line

The subject line give insight into the message the email contains. It can also hint at the outcome you would like. For example, if you are a business entrepreneur and you want to gain a contact as your client, the subject could be "I would love the opportunity to work with you!" This subject line is direct, grabs the reader's attention, and reaches out to him or her on a personal level.

Greeting

Formal greetings are more appropriate in a professional email than in their casual counterparts. "Hi" and "Dear" should be replaced with "Good afternoon" and "Good morning." Once you have chosen your greeting, it should be followed by the recipient's first name, without abbreviations and nicknames (even if you've met him or her already). Using his or her full name gives the recipient a sense of professionalism and pride. Using a truncated version of his or her name waters down that effect. You can witness the difference this makes when you're talking to a sales consultant. When she continues to use your first name, the amount of rapport she builds with you by default is greater than if she uses a truncated version.

Body of Text

Once you have greeted your recipient, reaffirm to him why you're sending the email and how you feel about him and/or his organisation. This should relate directly to your subject line and can be one or two sentences. The rest of the email should be brief and kept within a paragraph. Emails are a medium where the recipients expect the message to be short and sweet. Too much information will overload them, and they will begin to harvest negative thoughts towards you or your message.

Reread your email for grammar, spelling, and sentence structure. Such errors can cause your message to be interpreted differently from how you intend.

Call to Action/Thank You

After the body of your email, wrap up what you've said by mentioning your intention to get in contact with them, or leave it open for them to get in contact with you via your signature details. Thank them for their time.

Signature

Professional signatures can include organisation logos which are hyperlinked, direct and mobile numbers, website links, and links to social media platforms. If you are unemployed and do not have a default signature, you should construct one.

Signatures are used at the end of an email to identify the sender and provide the recipient with a means of getting in touch with him or her. Here is a basic format:

> Kind Regards,
> Natasha Hong
> M: 0401 222 656
> E: Natasha.hong12345@gmail.com

Send the Email

Once you've double-checked everything in the email, don't forget to attach any necessary documents. If attachments are included, RCI Success recommends mentioning the attachments in the email. This is so if the recipients have trouble opening them, did not notice them, or did not receive them, they will reply and advise you of this.

Once completed, send your email!

Voicemail

Setting up a Professional Voicemail

When you are actively job hunting, setting up a professional voicemail message is vital to ensuring you do not miss opportunities. Recruitment consultants are incredibly busy, and if they are not able to get in touch with you straight away or are unable to leave a voicemail message, they will turn to the next candidate in their shortlist.

With this in mind, they will also turn to the next candidate if your voicemail message is inappropriate or is not personalised.

Another point to consider is that you do not want to answer the phone in a busy and noisy environment, knowing the number could be that of a recruiter or a future employer's representative. Setting up voicemail gives you the luxury of returning phone calls when you're relaxed and in a comfortable environment where you can answer any questions recruiters have.

Now that you're convinced that having a professional voicemail is crucial, consider the following tips.

- *Keep it simple!* Provide a short message that tells callers they've reached the right voicemail by stating your name. Most people use "Hi, this is [name]. Sorry I'm not available at the moment, but please leave your name and number, and I'll get back to you as soon as I can."

- *Be clear and don't rush.* When you're recording your message, it needs to be at a calm pace. Be sure to replay the message before you apply it as your voicemail message. It may take multiple attempts before your message is clear and sounds professional.
- *Get another opinion.* To you, your message might sound clear and at a calm pace, but to another your message can sound as though you're anxious or can be hard to understand. Ask another to listen to your message and verify that it sounds professional.

Leaving a Professional Voicemail Message

When you're actively job searching, recruitment consultants and HR consultants of potential employers can leave you a voicemail message. Once you've listened to their message, it is within your best interested to return their phone call as soon as you can—preferably within one hour. Sometimes when you call back, you receive their own voicemail message. It is crucial to leave a professional voicemail message.

- *Acknowledge the person you're calling.* With your aim being to sound as professional as possible, greetings such as "Good morning" and "Good afternoon" are appropriate. These are recommended openings to your voicemail message.
- *Inform them of who you are.* This is simple. "This is Natalie Goodman, returning your phone call."
- *Explain why you've called.* Since you're returning their phone call, you can reiterate your interest in the current position advertised.
- *Ask for a call back.* "If you could, please contact me at [number]."
- *Thank them.*

Professional Telephone Manners

In roles with an emphasis on customer service, having an excellent telephone manner is crucial for you to be perceived by your colleagues, boss, and clients as professional. Your telephone manner will represent the business's image and is how organisations generate potential sales and maintain healthy relationships with clients.

Here are some suggestions for having a professional telephone manner. Adapt this approach to your company's needs or requirements.

- Always answer the telephone with your own name, your company name, and a question such as "How can I help you?" This confirms to the caller that he or she has been connected to the right person and/or organisation.
- When calling someone, always give your name and your business name at the start of the conversation. There is nothing worse than listening to someone talk on the telephone while not knowing to whom you are speaking and what it is regarding.
- At the beginning of the conversation, always give your reason for calling.
- Always try to be helpful to callers. If your business cannot provide them with what they want, try to suggest names of businesses which might. This adds to your image.
- If you have a voicemail bank set-up, make sure that the recorded message is clear and concise.
- Always respond to messages.

Now that you have the basics, you can use the phone etiquette below to effectively service your client's needs.

Some Things to Say	Some Things Not to Say
• Can I help you? • How can I help you? • May we be of any service? • May I take your name and address? • May I call you back later? • How can we assist you? • It's a pleasure. • Not a problem. • Thank you for calling. • Thank you for being so helpful. • Good morning/afternoon.	• Who? No, he is out. • No one told us. • I don't know when she'll be back. • Sorry, couldn't say. • Do you want someone else? • It's not my fault.

Understand Your Clients

If you do not understand your clients' needs and wants, it is difficult to build rapport and provide solutions to their problems. You must first understand the reason they have contacted your organisation and what responsibilities you have to service their needs. Grasping this means you can confidently build rapport with your clients.

By building rapport, you are establishing trust. You are listening to your client without interruptions, suggesting possible solutions, and making them feel confident in your ability to solve their problem or suggest a suitable product/service. If it is not in your capacity to help them immediately, inform them of your intention to seek assistance or answer their query as soon as possible. Keep them regularly updated on their case, and provide a reference number (if applicable) and your direct contact details (if allowed by your organisation).

Recommending Appropriate Services or Products

This section is especially useful for those in sales-related positions. When you adopt a consultative approach, how you structure your sentences, particularly at the beginning, are imperative. Beginning sentences with the phrases below invites clients to listen to your suggestions and express how they feel in response to these suggestions:

- "I suggest that you ..."
- "I encourage you to ..."
- "Here's what I propose ..."
- "I definitely recommend ..."
- "How would you feel about ...?"
- "Would you consider ...?"

Follow these through with open-ended questions—that is, questions that cannot be answered with a simple yes or no. These questions require answers with details and further explanation. A closed question is one like "Do you like driving in the rain?" which it can be answered with a yes or a no. An open-ended question such as "What do you think about the current government's budget cuts?" requires an answer supported by reasoning and deeper thinking. Using open-ended questions helps you further understand your clients and their needs and wants, thereby helping you satisfy their needs.

Phrases you should avoid

Some phrases sales professionals use irritate customers and do not inspire trust at all, though that is the professional's aim when using these phrases. Below is a list I have compiled from everyday encounters with salespeople over the telephone, as I enter a shop, or in email campaigns.

- "To be honest with you ..."
- "We offer the lowest price ..."
- "Lifetime guarantee."
- "You should ..."
- "Trust me."
- "I'm not sure. I'm not the decision-maker."
- "I don't know."
- "I understand."

I'm sure you have your own list of annoying phrases. Finding alternative phrases which are helpful and do not antagonise your clients is recommended so that professionalism is maintained and your organisation's reputation is enhanced rather than tarnished.

Cold Job Application Strategies

Cold job applications are for positions that are not currently advertised on behalf of the organisation and/or you are not enquiring in response to a position. You are contacting an organisation you have researched and hope they have a position or are willing to employ you. This approach requires confidence and determination. If mastered, it is a highly effective and a quick method of securing a job in an organisation of your choice.

This strategy requires a solid, methodical approach using a combination of professional emails or telephone calls for initial contacts, securing an interview or appointment with the decision-maker of the organisation, and following up if a position is not immediately available. Before making initial contact, ensure that your CV is up-to-date and you have all the documents that you believe are needed to secure employment.

1. Research the Organisation

Before you contact an organisation, make sure you thoroughly research it. You must be certain that you want to work for it, as the decision-makers will want to know your reasons for an approach. You need to display enthusiasm, knowledge of the organisation (its history and current projects), industry-related experience, or products that have recently been engaged or released onto the market.

2. Make an Initial Contact

Once you're comfortable with your decision, you need to make an initial contact. If possible, directly contact the decision-maker. For small businesses, this may the owner, a cofounder, or a business manager. For large corporate organisations, it is the HR manager or recruitment associate responsible for a particular division. Getting their direct contact details is vital so that your email or telephone is not wasted on gatekeepers: receptionists or PAs who filter unsolicited emails and phone calls.

If you are unable to find their direct contact details, unfortunately you must speak to the gatekeepers. For your call not to be lost or neglected, your approach must be tactful. You must keep in mind that decision-makers are busy, so it is unlikely you will be able to talk to them immediately regarding a position. If they are available, that's fantastic. Affirm your interest in working for them, and ask to arrange a suitable time when you can meet and talk about job prospects.

If you can't get contact information for a decision-maker, you will have to state your intentions to the gatekeepers and ask for that information. If they refuse to give it, ask them for an appropriate time to call back so you can speak to them personally. Try to avoid having them pass on a message. You don't want your interest to be swept under the rug. If this proves difficult, make a face-to-face appearance.

3. Make a Face-to-Face Appearance

If you choose this approach, you need to be thoroughly prepared to meet the decision-maker. You must dress in business attire, have a printed CV, and be ready for any questions.

Politely see the receptionist and tell her why you're there. Ask if the decision-maker is busy and has time to see you. If not, ask if he or she could make a time. If you sense that the receptionist is not comfortable with your approach (not all organisations are), politely ask if you could pass on a message and leave your CV.

4. Constructing an Email

Sending a professional email to the decision-maker directly or via a generic email requires a certain structure.

You must reach your recipient on a personal level. The subject line should identify the main reason for your email or the outcome you wish to achieve.

Address the recipient directly with a "Good afternoon" or "Good morning." Your next sentence should be a brief description about how you feel about the organisation and why you would like to work for it specifically.

The body of text should be a value proposition: what you as an individual can contribute to the organisation. This can range from your personal attributes, skills, and knowledge to your strong work ethic.

Make references to your attached CV and contact details. Thank the decision-maker for his or her consideration and once again communicate your enthusiasm by stating that you look forward to his or her response.

5. Follow Up the Email with a Telephone Call

Your aim is to get in contact with the decision-maker and make an appointment to discuss position opportunities. If your email is not responded to within three business days, you need to follow up with a phone call. This demonstrates your eagerness.

The demeanour in which you conduct yourself needs to be appropriate. You do not want to come across desperate—or worse, pushy. Calmly call the available number, let them know who you are and the reason for your call. Enquire as to whether they have received your email and if making an appointment at their convenience is an option. If there is resistance, don't be pushy. Thank them for their time, and wish them a great day.

Some gatekeepers have been instructed to respond to these phone calls in a certain manner, when the decision-maker is not open to this type of approach. Don't lose heart! There are many organisations which are open to it. Those that didn't give you a chance have just lost a great opportunity.

If you're able to land an appointment, congrats! You're almost there. Now you just have to be yourself and tell the decision-maker what you can contribute to the organisation.

6. Scheduled Appointment

Treat this as an interview. You need to be dressed to impress, punctual, and prepared. A guide on interview behaviour has been featured in Chapter 9: A Psychological Perspective.

Telephone Script Suggestions

Use this as a guide to engaging potential employers over the telephone. As something to hold in front of you while you speak, the script can help you project confidence and maintain professionalism.

When making a cold call, you can say the following:

"Good afternoon, [full name]. My name is [full name]. The reason for my call is that I would love the opportunity to work for [company name]. Do you have any positions available? Do you know who I can speak with regarding this?" From there you can start to elaborate on your ideal job role and previous work experience.

You need to speak with the decision-maker. If the receptionist asks to take a message, provide her with your contact details. You then need to ask when you would likely hear back from her or the decision-maker. This lets all know that you're eager and that you have every intention of following up.

If no one calls by a designated time, call the following day and say, "Good afternoon [name of person you spoke with], my name is [full name]. I spoke to you yesterday regarding my interest in working for your company. Were you able to get in touch with [name of decision-maker]?" This is what you need to say in order to determine whether the receptionist has forgotten. Whoever you liaise with might be forthcoming and state that they have no positions currently available. That's fine, but then ask if you could leave your CV, in case an opportunity arises.

Networking

Someone saying, "Look," is more powerful than someone saying, "Look at me."

Networking is one way to find job opportunities by making new contacts and starting new professional relationships which can help you and your organisation. For this method to be successful, there are strategies you need to use to ensure you do not come across as selfish and "contact hungry."

For some people, the prospect of approaching strangers and exchanging business cards or even starting a conversation is frightening. If you are one of them, it's okay; you do not have to start off with strangers. You can start by having successful conversations with your friends or people who have graduated from your university or high school. A sense of familiarity will put you at ease, and you can use this as a starting point.

When you meet someone, do not think that you are "networking." Think of it as an opportunity to meet new people, exchange information, and possibly help each other out in a business context. Inexperienced networkers who have networking on their mind are prone to apologise when they introduce themselves. This does not project a professional image and makes you seem as though you are not keen to build relationships.

You also do not have to pretend to be the life of the party to be a successful networker. Be yourself when you socialise with others. If you are not used to this, practise with a friend. Networking may require you to get out of your comfort zone, but that is a positive thing. Networking is the key to successful businesses.

If you're struggling to make new connections by yourself, ask people that you do know to politely introduce you to their connections or people they've met. This is a great way to be introduced without having to put in the initial groundwork.

Something you must remember is that great networking opportunities are present everywhere. Social events are not the only places where you can make a beneficial working relationship. Join clubs, go to industry-related events, and do anything where you can meet people and forge new connections.

Networking Follow-up

Once you've gathered your new contacts' business cards and reflected on the rapport you've built, you need to follow up with them. You can choose a phone call or an email. This is crucial for setting up beneficial relationships which can help you and your contact develop successful careers.

Invite your new contact to come to one of your organisation's events, social meetings, or volunteer services. These types of activities allow you to get to know them and build a relationship not based solely business. The invite itself is also thoughtful and demonstrates the way in which you welcome business—through relationships. These gestures are often reciprocated, which is great!

Top Job-Searching Strategy Tips

The following are pointers on what you should do when you are actively job searching.

1) *Always carry the following items,* such as personalised business cards (if you have them), a mini notepad, and a clean pen.
2) *Dress as though you might run into your next employer.* Always dress smart, be clean and groomed, and walk with confidence.
3) *Practise conversation starters.* If starting conversations with strangers is difficult, practise doing it before you meet with recruitment or HR consultants. This prevents awkward silences and the need to prepare "elevator topics." If you do not have time to practise, carry around conversation-starter cards in your pocket and memorise them so that they are at the forefront of your mind when you need them.
4) *Conduct your research.* When applying for jobs, conduct research regarding the company, its organisational culture, and opportunities for career progression. This will help you determine whether you want to work for them. It can also save time, as an

"organisational fit" is essential for a healthy employer-employee arrangement.

5) *Utilise job alerts.* When you register on employment websites such as SEEK.com or CareerOne, setting up job alerts based on filters can help narrow your job search. The websites will send you daily or weekly emails listing jobs according to your criteria. However, these alerts are renowned for being unreliable. Also, when you apply for a job, it is always best to be one of the first few to apply. This means you're at the top of the pile, and it expresses your enthusiasm to potential employers.

6) *Beware of scam job alerts.* Jobs that promise lucrative wages, flexible working hours, and home-based work are usually ploys to gain your personal information for identity or bank account theft. Be careful; always make sure advertised jobs originate from a trusted source.

7) *Check your social media profiles.* Employers are known for trying to locate candidates' social media profiles to gain a sense of who they are beyond their CVs and cover letters. To avoid discrimination, ensure that your profiles present you in a friendly and professional manner. Privacy settings need to restrict people outside your network from accessing your pictures, personal information, and timeline posts. A lot of people have lost job opportunities because of their profiles, so make sure that any previous drunken posts or complaints about your current or previous employers are not accessible to the public.

8) *Record and keep track of your job applications.*

Finding a Job Quickly

I'm going to explain my experiences between the November 9 and 22, 2013. I hope you will see why my approach was so successful and will learn how to apply a similar strategy to yourself. Please note that the reason this method was successful is due to the following.

I applied to jobs within the confines of my previous work experience and age.

- My first point of contact was professional.
- My second point of contact was professional.
- And my third point of contact was professional.

Every step was thought out; my approach was planned. This saved time and produced the results I wanted.

Saturday evening, November 9, I chose five job advertisements on SEEK to apply for. They were all temporary contract or part-time positions. They were positions for a sales technician, a recruitment assistant, an office administrator, an HR/payroll assistant, and a receptionist. Each position was from different industries and had very different job descriptions and prerequisites.

I took the time to draft an individual cover letter for each job and changed the points on my CV which were most important. I applied directly through SEEK and printed off each ad. I noted the date I applied for each job and had that information sitting in a neat pile on my desk. That was all I did.

Monday morning came, and I received a phone call for the sales technician role. Bob was very nice on the telephone. We briefly discussed my previous work experience, and then he asked me to meet him for an interview.

Tuesday morning came, and I received a phone call from a private number. I answered, and it was a man named Michael. We talked about the recruitment assistant position and how my previous work experience related to the job description. He asked why I would like to work in the HR division and that specific position. I mentioned details from the job description I'd printed off and why they interested me. He seemed pleased and said he would forward my details on to a client base, who would then decide if I progressed to the interview stage.

An hour after this phone call, another private number came up, and I answered, "Hello, Melissa speaking." It was Paul from a start-up recruitment agency boutique based in Castle Hill. And it was for the office administrator position. We talked about what I could offer, my availabilities, and if I could start immediately. Trying to determine my age, he strategically mentioned that his children attended Castle Hill High. He politely asked what year I graduated. Knowing what he was trying to do, I hesitated but obliged. He thanked me for my time and informed me that he will be in contact with me shortly.

I had three calls within two days. Since I applied to only five jobs, that gave me a call-back rate of 60 per cent. That is high!

Wednesday afternoon came, and I checked my email. The client of Michael, called Fred, referred to my previous conversation regarding the recruitment assistant role. In the body of his email, he stated that he would like to arrange an interview. He listed his availabilities in the email and asked me to contact him at my earliest convenience. At 4:30 p.m. Wednesday afternoon, I called Fred and organised an interview for Monday afternoon.

Let's take a pause from my story. Although it isn't the most interesting story, it does teach you a couple of things. First of all, there was no trick to getting callbacks. My first point of contact was tailored; my CV and cover letters were neat, and they were required in order to get a callback. Secondly, every time I engaged a potential employer or a decision-maker, I was professional and effectively communicated what I could offer his or her organisation in terms of my skills, ability, and work ethic.

Now that you have seen there is no magic to my success, you should agree that this type of efficiency comes with practise and knowing what to do and what not to do. It initially requires a lot of effort, and that effort does bear fruit quite quickly. Now back to my story ...

It was the eighteenth of November, a Monday afternoon, and it was bucketing rain. I was not keen for an interview. Nevertheless, I put my enthusiastic mask on, and off I went. I gave myself a window of twenty minutes for "getting lost" time, as I had never driven to that area. I thought it wouldn't be me if I took an umbrella, so I didn't. When I arrived, I got into the elevator, I adjusted my clothes, wiped my glasses, and fixed my hair. Elevators with mirrors are the absolute best. It saved me a trip to the bathroom.

I greeted the receptionist, took a seat, and soon after was interviewed. The interviewer was very friendly and had a firm handshake and a nice big smile. When we were seated in the interview room, he asked what I liked the most about my previous role (as it was the most relevant to the job). I wasn't prepared for that question, and I paused to gather my thoughts. This reduced the amount of ums, but I wasn't pleased with my response. With some tough questions and the cosy room, I began to sweat. I hate it when that happens.

I thanked him for his time and shook his hand. He said he would be in touch the next day. He didn't get in touch.

On the twenty-second of November, I got a call from a woman asking me to come in for an interview. I asked her to email me the address, and I organised a suitable time. On the interview day, I got incredibly lost, as it was another area I was unfamiliar with. I called ten minutes before the interview time and informed them of this. They understood and provided me with fresh directions.

I walked in and was introduced to their small team. All three of them had decided to interview me simultaneously. I sat facing all of them and made a mental note to engage all of them with eye contact. The middle man talked the most, while the other two took notes.

Starting off the interview, they made note that I was the first one they were interviewing. For most, this would put pressure on, but I knew it was advantageous. When you process new information, your memory stores the first and last blocks of information most efficiently. The middle is often difficult to recollect and doesn't form as prominent an impression on the mind as the beginning and end. Therefore, being interviewed first, I was automatically going to imprint a stronger impression on their minds. It was my aim to make that impression a positive one.

They went through my CV and asked some standard questions. They also explained why the role was available. I asked some questions in return. Afterwards they said they would be in touch early the next week … and so they were!

Two reference checks later, I was reading a letter of offer, and I started the following week.

From these experiences, it's apparent there is an art to finding a job quickly. You need to play by your strengths and know which jobs you are and are not suited to. Target these jobs with your first line of attack: your tailored CV and cover letters. Reaffirm in their minds that you're suitable through your professional telephone rapport, and land the job from a great interview.

Now that you know the strategy, go and practise! If I can get a job, why can't you?

Utilising Social Media to Project the Right Image

With the emergence of advanced technology, social media has become an inexpensive platform for many businesses to gain vast exposure. They utilise social media for marketing, networking, and generating potential dealer relationships, clients, and customer bases. These platforms can also be utilised by eager candidates during their job searches. You should also note that they are regularly used by employers and recruitment agencies in their selection processes.

Boutique recruitment agencies commonly utilise Fb (Facebook) to determine whether a candidate might fit a job specification. Large recruitment agencies are governed by bodies which enforce antidiscrimination legislation, prohibiting employment selection based on sex, gender, appearance, or location. Using the details provided in résumés, agencies look up candidates on Fb. The candidates' profiles—how they dress, what type of activities they enjoy, whether they seem to like to party or club too much—can be the determining factor in whether they are invited to an interview.

This disregards candidate's competencies and is a direct violation of the antidiscrimination act.

With these processes being unsolicited, it is the candidates' responsibility that their Fb profiles are not detrimental to any of their job applications. Precautions can be taken.

- Increase the privacy settings on your profile. Those who are not friends should be limited from viewing your personal information, such as your birthday, where you live, the school you are or have attended, and the year you graduated from high school.
- Access to your photos should be blocked to strangers. If you do not feel this is necessary, it is best to screen your photos. Drunken and sexually explicit photos should be available only to friends or removed from your profile.

Taking these actions can limit the discrimination carried out by boutique recruitment agencies in their selection process.

Due to the networking nature of Fb, candidates can utilise this to connect with potential employers and become exposed to more job opportunities.

LinkedIn

LinkedIn is a fantastic social platform for maintaining relationships and creating new ones. These can be both social and business contacts. You can build your profile so that you are found when employers search for specific words. You can also use the free account or pay for a premium membership so that LinkedIn acts as your virtual portfolio.

I've included some tips below to maximise the chances of employers finding you to fill a job role.

Your profile picture should not be the standard of the one you use on Facebook. It must have a professional look or be professionally taken by a photographer. Front-on, black and white photos are commonly used. Women should have their makeup done with natural tones and their hair up so that it does not covering any aspect of your face. Fringes should be pinned back or styled off the face. Men with long hair should have it pulled back and their hair styled; this can include combed back or gelled.

Your header should be your current or most recent position. This is what employers search for. They also search by location and use multiple filters. Your location can be noted on your profile.

Indicate the type of industry you've had experience in, whether it is HR, leisure, or wholesale goods.

Next, treat your account as a CV. You need to include your previous work, volunteer experience, and significant achievements in chronological order under the appropriate headings.

- Job title, role, period of employment
- A thorough job description
- Achievements
- A paragraph reference from a colleague, supervisor, or manager
- Ask colleagues or your supervisor to endorse your skills listed at the bottom of your profile. *Note:* If they endorse you, it is common courtesy to return the favour.

Your job description must incorporate KPIs you complied with, what duties you were responsible for, whom you reported to, and your day-to-day activity. Neat and concise presentation is key. Bullet points are recommended. A small paragraph describing your major achievements (if any) during your period of employment is great for impressing potential employers.

LinkedIn for Business

LinkedIn is a free resource which can form a major component of your free business marketing campaign. By creating a company page and linking it to your own profile, you can successfully generate business exposure.

Following the steps below will enhance your LinkedIn marketing campaign.

1. Gather as many useful connections as possible. These can be your classmates, colleagues, people you've just met at a networking function, or people you are seeking to connect with professionally.

2. Use recommendations on LinkedIn. These should outline the quality of your services or products, how you conduct yourself professionally, and how pleased they were in their dealings with you. These type of reviews garner trust and credibility in the public eye and encourage others to engage your services or utilise your products.

3. Utilise LinkedIn search to follow other companies similar to yours. This serves as a means to track your competition and compare your own page's success with theirs.

4. Posting regular updates, blogs, or discussion topics allows you to interact with your target clients. It reminds them of your existence and creates the opportunity for them to provide you feedback on your services or products. Feedback should be encouraged!

5. Join groups related to your industry or business. Actively participate in their discussion forums, and note the type of professionals interested in these discussions. These members could be your next clients.

6. Send messages to other professionals within the same LinkedIn groups as you. These message can be a brief introduction of you as a professional, your own business, and what you can offer them. Also invite them to follow your company page. Be careful not to harass people.

7. In the topic area on LinkedIn, provide answers to their questions. You can then refer them to your own company page for further information or give them permission to contact you personally if they require further elaboration. Helping others first is the best way for people to help you and your business grow.

8. Businesses utilise LinkedIn as an effective advertising board. The price for advertising relative to LinkedIn's exposure level is quite

low and should be seriously considered once money is allocated towards a business marketing campaign.

9. If you are impressed by LinkedIn and what it can do for you professionally or for your business, you can upgrade your account to a paid membership. Three different membership levels are available.

The great thing about LinkedIn is that it is simple and user-friendly. You do not have to hire a professional to set up your business marketing campaign. You are quite capable yourself!

Internships

Internships are very different from jobs. A job is designed for the worker to perform and benefit the organisation and in exchange to receive monetary compensation. The purpose of an internship is to encourage learning and quite often provides an entry-level graduate or student the opportunity to gain work experience. Internships can be unpaid or paid and have a designated duration. However, some organisations take advantage of students eager to gain work experience. They pigeonhole the students, giving them mundane tasks such as data entry, filing, and responding to emails. This does not encourage growth and inhibits industry-related learning. It is your responsibility to ensure that your internship enriches your learning experience.

It has been found that smaller and new upcoming businesses are more willing to teach interns and give them a wide range of tasks. Large corporations are capable of this only when intern programs have been designed and implemented by their HR divisions.

Now that you understand the differences between a job and an internship, you can understand why the method in which you apply to an internship also differs. The process can be either more complex or simple, depending upon the industry and size of the organisation.

Example 1

A non-profit organisation offers two internship placements a year. Its process includes applying to the job advertisement with a cover letter and CV and attending a face-to-face interview. The internship duties and responsibilities are very broad and not specific.

Example 2

A large company's summer internship program has five steps to undertake:

1. Registering on the company's website and filling out an extensive application form including details of previous work experience, academic transcripts, and GPA average, and your reasons for wanting to undertake the internship
2. A telephone interview enquiring as to what skills and knowledge were gained from your previous work or volunteer experience and the reasons you undertook those roles
3. Tests including an aptitude and psychological test over the Internet, testing mathematical and reasoning ability, and cognitive functioning
4. An interview with the company's HR consultant
5. An interview with the branch manager

The job description is extensively detailed; it provides information on areas of involvement, the duration of each division the intern will stay in, tasks and responsibilities, and the overseeing manager's name.

With the structure and internship design varying enormously, you as an intern need to decide whether you prefer highly structured learning or flexibility; an area of interest can be learnt more thoroughly. Once you've decided this, your application approach must be altered.

Here is an invitation to complete an online assessment in order to be eligible for a 2013 internship programme:

> *Dear Monica,*
>
> *Congratulations on being selected to take part in the online aptitude assessment for the Company Y Internship Programme. This will involve you completing an online ability test. This will involve numerical reasoning and logical reasoning. Please note that you will need to complete this by midday AEST, 28 July.*
>
> *You will be able to complete a practise test in order to prepare yourself before taking each test.*
>
> *In order to complete the test, please follow the instructions below.*

Following are the Company Summer Internship Programme details:

> *Your interview will last approximately thirty to forty-five minutes and will be an opportunity for you to discuss*
>
> - *your experience and skills;*
> - *why you want to work for [company name]; and*
> - *why you are interested in our Intern Programme and Role.*
>
> *You will also be asked a few behavioural-based questions.*
>
> *Good luck!*

Hiring Manager Name:	_____
Intern Position Title:	*[Company] Admin Support*
Intake:	*Early March*
Duration:	*12 months*
Project Area Description:	*Supporting Product X Accounts*
Internal Job Description:	
Tech Skills/Knowledge	*General Comp skills. MS Office: Excel, PP, Word*
Non-Tech Skills/Knowledge	*Problem solving, excellent written and verbal communication skills, able to work in a large business environment*

Nonspecific internship descriptions allow you flexibility in your learning, and you can thereby become involved in various areas of a business. Below is an example of a job description for a flexible internship opportunity.

Skills

- Computer savvy
- Able to think outside the square and solve problems
- Have an eye for detail and problem solving
- Able to liaise professionally with clients
- Outstanding verbal, written, and interpersonal skills
- Confident with all social media platforms: Facebook, Twitter, Pinterest, and Instagram
- Must be creative, passionate, and hard-working
- Well presented
- Have good knowledge of and interest in brands

Role parameters

- Research and compose blog posts—requires exceptional writing skills.
- Assist with newsletter composition.

- Book and follow up on couriers.
- Control stock.
- Learn the functionality of the business: order process, marketing, and business development.
- Work in the back end of our website.
- Assist with photo shoot planning and styling.
- Do general ad-hoc duties.

Successful internship placements can often lead to a letter of offer when the organisation is satisfied with the interns' performance and would like him or her to occupy a permanent paid position.

Telephone Screening Templates

Some small organisations with less structured internship selection processes use screening templates to help make their decisions.

Criteria
Motivation Tell us a little about yourself? What are you studying? Why do you want to undertake an internship? What drew you to apply for this particular internship?
IT skills and competencies Photoshop, MS programs, blogging, Word Press Social media: Online forums, Myspace, Facebook, LinkedIn, podcasts, Twitter, Instagram Accounting software
Experience What was your role at _____? What type of skills did you gain from that experience?
Career progression Where do you see yourself five years from now? How do you think this internship will benefit you in terms of where you want to go?

Personality Do you consider yourself a self-starter? Why? Do you work well unsupervised? Give an example. What's something unique you could contribute?	
Availability/commitment (minimum three months) How many days and/or hours are you willing to commit? How would you travel? Do you own a car?	
Resources Do you have your own computer?	

Interview Question Template

JD Requirement	Questions
Personality Self-starter, proactive, creative, career-driven/ hard-working	*Icebreakers* Tell us a bit about yourself: hobbies, interests? What's one of your most rewarding experiences? *Career* What do you hope to gain from this internship? What would you like to accomplish in the next year? What do you aim to learn once you graduate? What's your motivation?
Communication skills Email/telephone, written	Have you had experience using the telephone or email to follow up or communicate with customers or clients? Can you provide an example when a high level of communication was required to resolve a problem? How did you go about resolving the issue?
Social media/IT MS programs, blogging, PR	Do you use social media regularly? Do you use them confidently? Do you blog?

	MS Office Have you used Excel for data entry? Conducted BD calls, research? Are you confident using Word, Outlook?
Skills	What do you believe to be your greatest strengths and weaknesses? How do you go about managing your weaknesses? Do you excel in any areas, whether that is IT, writing, sales, research, networking?
Company	What's something you believe you can contribute to our family-owned business?

These template questions are not as concise as ones for larger organisations. They do not have a systematic method of assessing applicants' answers. Comments and notes are taken down while listening, but these cannot be weighted to compare each applicant effectively. This is a disadvantage of more-flexible internships.

Free Courses Online

Undertaking online courses is a great way to reinforce the skills you are learning in your job. It is also a way to gain an understanding of areas in which you have no knowledge or need to refresh what you have previously learnt.

Become a participant in research panels on projects and/or marketing surveys. Joining research and marketing groups is a great way to earn extra cash while you look for employment. Rewards can come in the form of gift cards, credit points to an account, or payment. Examples include the Roy Morgan Business Panel and Farron Research.

You can also include your participation on your CV. It demonstrates that you're able to communicate your opinion and work in groups (common in market research).

Online Courses Requiring Payment

A lot of junior roles require a certain skill set. And many small businesses require candidates to have basic customer-service skills, administration capabilities, and competence dealing with ad-hoc duties. One way to get an edge over other junior candidates is to gain certifications which prove your competencies. This can range from enrolling in basic, intermediate, or advanced online classes which teach MS programs or accountancy programs such as MYOB or Xero, which small businesses use for payroll, invoicing, and managing stock inventory. These courses provide step-by-step instructions on how to navigate programs and ways of refining and improving computer skills.

If you're looking for a casual job, such as part-time work in a bar, club, or another premise which serves alcohol, it would be wise to attain an RSA and/or RCG. This allows you to serve alcohol (RSA) and work in a gambling environment (RCG). You must be over the age of eighteen to become certified. These courses are easy to pass; they are one-day workshops with all the answers provided in a handout. After completion of the workshop, one assessment is conducted, and all you need to do is pass. The price usually ranges between fifty and one hundred dollars for each certificate. Combo details are available.

When offered by high schools, these courses offered are often free. Note that RSA and RCG certificates expire every three years and require recertification.

Retain all certificates for your portfolio, which you take to interviews.

University or College Social Groups or Clubs

This kind of involvement provides a glimpse into your personality, interests, and leadership abilities. It's a fantastic opportunity to meet people who share your interests and to occupy a role which challenges you. For example, being a general executive in the Psychology Society means you need to coordinate the annual cruise party, Halloween party, monthly barbecue, and bar events. This requires organisation, promotion, delegating tasks to other coordinators, and working with a team.

Your personal responsibilities and any major events you organised and assisted with a society or club should be included in your CV.

Using Referees and References

It is your responsibility to ensure your written references are correct, reflect your period of employment or volunteer experience, and are useful for your future job search.

The written reference below lacks detail; it does not elaborate on the duties and responsibilities, or show the period and the location of volunteering.

LOGO

1/11/_____

To Whom It May Concern:

Please accept this reference for Melissa_____.

Melissa has been volunteering her services since 24 May, _____.

During her time with us, Melissa has always presented herself in a respectful and positive manner within the house and engaged very well with the range of people who come through the door.

Unfortunately due to study commitments, Melissa has become unavailable to volunteer with us, and it is our hope that she will be able to return at a later stage.

I would recommend Melissa to any future employer.

Please feel free to contact me if you have any further queries

Below is an example of a positive written reference. Compare this to the previous example.

[logo]

COMPANY NAME

Unit 28 No. 11, Luxley Drive

Cranebrook VIC 2334 Australia

Tel: (02) 9859 2119 Fax: (02) 9111 1122

Email: *info@farandwider.com.au*

Website: *www.southerlyandpacific.com.au*

ABN: 63 0798 910 288

11 June, 2014

To whom it may concern,

I confirm that Melissa was employed by Far and Wider Pty Ltd as a Sales Consultant from _____ to _____.

It is my pleasure to recommend Melissa _____, as her performance working as a project manager for Far and Wider Pty Ltd proved that she would be a valuable addition to any company.

I have known Monica for 16 months in my capacity as the owner and manager at Far and Wider Pty Ltd. Monica worked for me, undertaking numerous tasks, such as rewriting the Administration Manual for technical, administration, and finance/accounting, updating the website monthly, and researching target markets to generate potential customers.

Monica distinguished herself by taking initiative daily to improve the company's productivity. Monica was always punctual, hard working, driven, and determined to go beyond what her job required of her.

Monica is highly intelligent and has substantial analytical and communication skills. She used this to her advantage in developing new marketing ideas in our XYZ Product Drive project.

If her performance in our company is any indication of how she would perform in your company, she would be a great asset.

It was unfortunate her employment with us had to end following a strategic review of the company's positions.

We wish her all the best in her future endeavours.

Volunteering

Volunteering is a great way to gain work experience while giving back to the community. This can be a first step for those who have never had a job and need to build their CV. When undertaking volunteer roles, it is necessary to gain transferable skills—skills which can be used and recognised by potential employers when seeking candidates. It is also wise to seek volunteer experience in your future career industry. For example, if you wish to become a registered psychologist, volunteering for a non-profit which specialises in mental health recovery could provide exposure to those suffering from bipolar disorder, schizophrenia, or chronic depression. Volunteer experience can also be enlightening, showing yourself new areas of interest and perhaps even that your ideal career is not what you originally expected.

Most agencies will recognise your contributions and issue certificates of thanks. Keep these, and include copies of them in your CV folder as proof of your experience. You should keep copies of all your certificates.

Small Organisations vs. Large Organisations

When you're looking for a job, it is crucial to be aware of the type of organisation you are suited to. Large corporations have a significantly different working culture and environment than their small business counterparts or competition. Understanding these differences and their associated advantages and disadvantages will help you decide whether you want to target large corporations or small local businesses.

Small Organisations

The size of an organisation is determined by the number of employees. A small business is between one and ten employees, whilst a small to medium organisation is between eleven and twenty. Once an organisation goes over twenty employees, it becomes a Category 1 employer. This requires it to have implemented HR policies and procedures, and standardised working practises.

Advantages:

- In a small organisation, employees have greater job flexibility. Job descriptions are not clearly defined, and people are endowed with various responsibilities. This gives you the opportunity to be challenged continually and to learn in areas you may not be familiar with.
- A close-knit working culture and team is formed. All employees know each other, and you can build strong working relationships within your team. If one person is not pulling his or her weight, it is very noticeable.
- Individual employees have a stronger voice than those in larger corporations. What they contribute to building the business is valued and acknowledged.
- Problems are immediately discussed within the team or with the manager. Corrective action is often immediate, and the entire team is included in providing a solution or monitoring improvements.

Disadvantages:

- With fluid job descriptions, the boundaries regarding who is responsible for what task or target become blurred. Communication between team members is essential for tasks to be completed by their deadlines.
- Smaller organisations expect workers not just to clock in and clock out. If you are to fit into a small organisational culture, it is expected that you be willing to put in extra hours to complete work and help out others. Everyone must work together, and if you are seen as only "working for the money," you will not be employed for long.
- The pay rates of employees are based solely on the discretion of the manager or owner of the business. Salary decisions do not involve a board of directors, a team of HR personnel, or a CEO. Commonly, inconsistencies arise, and feuds can brew between employees who perform similar tasks if huge pay gaps exist.

Large Corporations

In large organisations, strict HR policies and procedures are established. These can include workers' health and safety, performance appraisals, learning and development programs, grievance and privacy policies, employee contracts, and rigid job descriptions with incorporated KPIs and responsibilities. With an enormous amount of information transparency, all employees have no excuse for not knowing what is expected of them in terms of performance and organisational behaviour towards clients and other employees.

Advantages:

- Within multinational corporations, multiple working divisions or departments exist. This presents employees with internal career-progression opportunities. Travelling oversees by becoming an expatriate is not available within smaller organisations.

- Pay scale and reasons for pay rises, pay cuts, and redundancies are justified by statistics, budget reports, and different levels of management.
- With explicit job descriptions, employees do not feel confused about the roles they are to undertake daily. A daily routine is formed and creates a structure which is followed; this eases assimilation into a new company.

Disadvantages:

- Rigid job descriptions mean little flexibility exists for employees to deviate from their set tasks and responsibilities. Deviations in large corporations are met with disciplinary action.
- With internal career-progression opportunities being limited, competition between employees for a position can tarnish working relationships.
- Internal department competition can also happen when rewards are given to the department which reaches a target first. Negative working relationships soon develop, leading to departments which do not communicate with one another.
- The rate at which an organisation grows is dependent on the organisational culture and whether continuous innovation via the contribution of unique ideas from their employees is encouraged or discouraged. This can be frustrating for people who crave change or find it exciting. For other types of employees, this could be an advantage as they do not feel pressured to contribute innovations.
- Individual employee voices are limited. Any changes made or in the planning stage must be preapproved by various levels of management. Any immediate problem must be discussed with managers via a scheduled appointment. This can delay corrective action.

These are the basic differences between large and small organisations. They neglect the major operational, economic, and social issues incorporated within each structure. Bear this in mind when you decide to pursue employment within a small or large organisation.

Start-Up Organisations

Has it ever come across your mind to target start-up companies for employment opportunities? If it hasn't, you may consider start-ups as a suitable option after reading the advantages associated joining an organisation at the very beginning.

Advantages:

- Start-up organisations are looking for employees! At the very beginning, the owners or managing directors are searching for their first few employees to build their company. They need high-quality assistance quickly and will continue to recruit until they find the "right" people.

- Start-ups understand that their first few employees set the benchmarks and directions of their organisation. Workers' personalities will mould the organisation's culture, so directors try to find workers who are able to put forward their own unique contribution. Understanding this, you should target start-up organisations if you are the type of person to put in the extra effort and to be loyal to an organisation with an uncertain future and insecure employment.

- Within a start-up, the owners or managing directors are too busy to micromanage their new employees. They delegate tasks and must allow employees the freedom and ability to utilise their creativity. This is suitable to those who find it frustrating to have someone constantly peeking over their shoulder.

- In a start-up, there are no clearly defined job descriptions. Job roles overlap, and everyone must work together to achieve common short-term goals to grow the company. Wearing multiple hats is a great opportunity for those who do not like being pigeon-holed—being limited in the job tasks and responsibilities they undertake daily.

- In start-ups, open communication between all levels of management is essential. As a small, close-knit team, it is essential for business functioning that all levels of management communicate openly. The overlap of job descriptions encourages the team to differentiate who is responsible for certain tasks and set deadlines. This requires open lines of communication and a respect amongst colleagues regardless of organisational status.

- Working in a small team for thirty-eight hours or more a week (if you're full time) can lead to developing strong co-worker relationships. You rely on one another to complete your tasks and consult on the best ways to complete tasks; as systems and procedures are either being developed or must be created from scratch. As a team, you also feel a sense of accomplishment when a difficult project is completed or a new system has been implemented and you witness its impact on the company's growth. As you share these accomplishments, strong relationships can be forged.

- These strong working relationships can be great contacts for you if you were to begin your own start-up company. They might join you as partners, offer assistance, or recommend suitable employees.

- If one person in a small team was to become lazy or rely on other team members to pick up the slack, it becomes obvious to the rest of the team. Employees who do not maintain an expected productivity level do not suit a start-up company.

- Your achievements will be quite noticeable. The effect of your achievements and hard work will directly impact your team's work, daily routine, and targets.

- You will learn, and learn rapidly. A start-up company does not always have a set way of solving problems or providing services or products which specifically address clients' needs. Quite often you will face a unique problem the company has never faced, and it will be up to you find a solution. You will regularly conduct research for innovative solutions, methods of improving or designing systems and procedures to implement. In turn, you will learn rapidly and expand upon your current skill set and knowledge.

Disadvantage:

- Because a start-up's future is uncertain, there is no job security. Soon after you are hired, you may find that they are unable to keep paying you or that your position has been deemed unnecessary. However, if you remain loyal and stay with the company through its financial hardship, you may be greatly rewarded in the future. This may include assuming a management position and an associated pay rise in the future.

- Sometimes working in a start-up is like living in a small town. This is not an issue for employees who enjoy working on a team. But those who work best solo and without regular collaboration can find this a frustrating component of their work. If working independently is something you value highly, joining a start-up may prove to be a challenge.

- Constant change is a key characteristic of start-ups. This is not a disadvantage to people who embrace continual change. However, a lot of people find constant change uncomfortable; it makes them feel uneasy. These people experience anxiety in their job role when they do not know what to expect when they arrive at work every day. You need to know whether this would be a potential issue if you were to work for a start-up.

To Join a Start-Up or Not to Join a Start-Up

Now that you have been informed about the advantages and disadvantages of joining a start-up company, you can begin to make an informed decision about whether you would like to work for one. Before making a decision, you should ask some of these questions:

- *How do the founders know each other?* You want to know the extent of the founders' relationship, as this will determine whether they will cooperate and reach a solution in times of difficulty and financial hardship.
- *What is the ultimate goal for the company and the founders?* You need to know how your job fits into their long-term goals. With

start-ups, the business model or plan continually evolves, and if your skills are not in demand for the long term, it is a risk to join up with them.

- *What's in it for you?* If you are going to be working long hours to help the founders achieve their goals, you need to know what your reward is. Will you be granted a major pay increase once systems are established or the company has reached a major milestone?
- *What is the company's focus for the next three months?* If the founders or the interviewers cannot give you a concise answer, your alarm bells should be set off. A clear direction is a bare minimum to becoming and remaining a successful start-up. If they also provide an answer which does not include your job role, question more deeply. You need to know where your role fits in the grand scheme of their business model.
- *What are the organisation's main competitors?* Their attitude when they answer this indicates whether they acknowledge their competitors' existence and/or know a lot about them and how their organisation differentiates itself.

The above questions are mere suggestions. Asking these and more specific questions before you join a start-up are necessary; you must completely understand the risks and rewards associated with a start-up before making your decision.

Do I Tell My Boss I'm Looking for Other Work?

A lot of us struggle with this question. Some of us believe it is a common courtesy to let management know of your intentions to leave. Some feel that you shouldn't tell them, as your employers may feel as though it is a personal betrayal and turn nasty. So do you tell them, or do you keep your intentions to yourself?

In my opinion, it is not a good idea to tell your boss that you're looking elsewhere. You may posit that you have a great relationship with your boss, and he or she will understand the reasons for your departure. You may even posit that it will help management prepare for your departure, as they can initiate recruitment and selection practises to find your replacement. What I offer is a contrasting perspective that is just as valid. I invite you to develop your own opinion and make your own decision once you cross this bridge.

First, if you tell your employer that you are leaving before you have secured your next working venture, I believe you have dug your own grave. You have lost the opportunity for promotions. Also, if you considered your relationship with your boss to be great or if you are more than just collaborative professionals, you will soon find out that your relationship dynamic has shifted.

Your managers will limit your involvement in future projects; they will believe that it is best that you are not involved so it is easier for job delegations and sharing your workload once you leave. Your colleagues and other layers of management may see you as a traitor and start treating you differently. You may not be invited to meetings, and your opinion may become unwanted, no matter how valid your points are.

I recommend not telling your colleagues that you intend on leaving. My main reason is this: you do not want your boss to hear that you're leaving from someone other than you. You may seem deceitful and dishonest to upper management. Your boss should be the first to know that you're leaving or have been offered alternative employment. Then, by all means, inform your colleagues of your departure.

How Do I Leave on a Positive Note?

As soon as you have the revelation that you're no longer happy working in your current job, whether that is because of a pretentious boss, poor pay, or a rigorous workload, take immediate action to change your situation. It is not conducive to your mental and emotional well-being to be in an occupation which only causes you grief.

Some people have the attitude that they must "stick it out." Although this is a noble concept, starting the process of job hunting when unhappy denotes decisiveness and should be viewed as a positive thing. Waiting it out is not helpful to you or your family; although your family may be dependent upon your income, they experience the ancillary effects of your stress. With this in mind, changing jobs can be positive not only for you, but also your family. (If you're not in the financial position to change jobs, this approach is not recommended.)

Once you've made the major decision to change jobs, you need to form a game plan of how to leave. This can make the difference between receiving a positive or a negative reference.

Informing Your Boss that You're Leaving

The mode in which you inform your boss about your decision to resign is key. The most appropriate method is asking your boss in advance for a scheduled time when you and your boss talk. This initiation can be either face-to-face or via email. You don't have to elaborate on the reasons for this scheduled time, you just need to make the time and ensure that it is sufficient. Your boss may have questions about why you've made your decision and if there is anything they can do to convince you to stay.

Asking for sufficient time allows your boss to assess the seriousness of your period of notice and any form of remuneration or annual leave. Unless you're adamant in your decision, give your boss this time. There may be something you haven't considered that would keep you there.

Resigning

Resigning must be face-to-face. There is nothing worse than people resigning over the phone or via email. Even if you're in your probation period and feel as though you do not owe your employer any form of loyalty or consideration, this is not recommended. Whenever you leave an employer, ensure that you leave on a positive note. You do not want them to hold negative opinions of you or regret hiring you.

To ensure that your boss does not take your resignation personally or as a reflection on their leadership or employment standards (although that might be the reason), you need to have a face-to-face discussion.

Discussion

During your meeting, you must do the following:

- Outline the reason for your meeting: your resignation.
- Outline the reasons you're leaving.
- Indicate that this is your period of notice and hand in your signed resignation letter. *Keep a copy for yourself!*
- Allow your boss to absorb what you have said, and allow him or her to direct the rest of the meeting until it ends.

Resignation Letter

In essence, a resignation letter must maintain a high standard of professionalism. This can be difficult if the decision sparks strong emotions, which could range from anger to relief, with a shedding of a few tears. Consider these points when writing your letter:

- Your boss and other forms of management (if they exist) will read your letter. Therefore it must be polite, concise, and detailed as to why you are leaving.
- Proofread your letter. Make sure there is nothing you've neglected and that you are conveying the right message to your boss.
- The length of your letter will vary depending on the size of your company and your reasons for leaving. For example, if you work in a large corporation, you may be required to send it to the HR department, in which case your letter needs to be formal and brief.

Smaller organisations may not even require a letter. But if your boss is the owner, he or she would appreciate a letter elaborating your reasons. Short letters can be viewed as offensive.

Here is an example of a formal resignation letter:

28 September, 2013

Ms Melanie Humack

Recruitment Associate

Melo HR

101 Dalmation Road

Diagon Alleville, NSW 2116

Dear Aimee Moody,

I am writing to inform you that I will be resigning from my position as HR associate. The reason for my resignation is that I have been offered another position in Realtime HR. This position incorporates more responsibilities and acts as an opportunity to further my career. Unfortunately, this means I am unable to continue my work at Melo HR.

As stated in my contract, it is required that I provide two weeks' notice. Please consider this letter as my notice, with my last day being the 5 October, 2013.

After my resignation, if you have any queries regarding the work I have undertaken, feel free to contact me on 0401 888 789 or email me at melanie.humack45@gmail.com

I regret any inconvenience my resignation may cause.

An Easy Transition

Upon leaving, if possible, you should take it upon yourself to help the new employee understand the tasks and workload you are leaving behind.

This is not only courteous, but it makes the transition easier for your boss; training and inductions are easier when the line between completed and uncompleted work is clear. This eases stress to your boss or your team and helps ensure you leave on a positive note.

Make this transition easier by making sure your work environment is tidy, organised, and accessible to anyone without prior company knowledge. For example, set up your files according to the company manual, not your own personalised system. You can also write a brief with instructions and details about your current projects or work so that these can be completed and the structure of each task/project is consistent. Also brief your boss regarding the progress of each project or any urgent/outstanding work that needs to be addressed within your last few days of departure.

Now That You've Left

Congratulations! Now that you have resigned, you can move on to bigger and better things. If you're resigning without a guaranteed job, don't lose hope if you struggle to find a new job. One of the worst things you can do is go back to a company where you've resigned due to stress, bullying, or overwhelming working conditions. There is a reason you left, and don't forget it. Chin up, keep trying, and remember that your emotional and physical well-being not only affect you but also your family.

You've Been Chosen! Now What?

You've landed a job, and you're over the moon about it. So how do you get started? Whenever a new employee is inducted into an organisation in Australia, a few standard documents must be signed and provided before work commences. These documents include the following:

- Tax File Declaration form
- Choice of Super form
- Ombudsman Fair Work information statement
- Letter of offer with an attached job description

Tax File Declaration Form

This document is available at newsagencies for free around Australia. They are to be filled out by employees before their first payslip is issued. Your tax file number (TFN) is the equivalent of a Social Security number. It identifies you to the Australian Taxation Office (ATO) and allows the government to monitor how much money you earn annually, how much tax you owe, and the amount of superannuation you are entitled to from your employer.

The following information is required for form completion:

- Full name
- Date of birth
- Full address
- TFN
- Claiming tax-free threshold, declaration of any debts, HECS-HELP
- Citizenship status

Once both the employee and the employer complete the form, it is lodged to the ATO by the employer.

Choice of Super Form

This is a form issued by the ATO. It has two chapters: one is for you, the employee, and the other is for the employer to complete. This form allows you to allocate your own superannuation account for your new employer to make contributions towards at every pay cycle. It also gives you the option to use the employer's choice of fund. In this form you must provide your TFN.

If you require more information about this form, visit www.ato.gov.au.

Ombudsman Fair Work Information Statement

This outlines every employee's rights according to the Fair Work Act 2009, which includes ten National Employment Standards (NES). The NES are the minimum standards and entitlements of all employees:

1) A maximum standard working week of thirty-eight hours for full-time employees, plus "reasonable" additional hours.
2) A right to request flexible working arrangements.
3) Parental and adoption leave of twelve months (unpaid), with a right to request an additional twelve months.
4) Four weeks paid annual leave each year (pro rata).
5) Ten days paid compassionate leave for each permissible occasion, and two days unpaid carer's leave for each permissible occasion.
6) Community service leave for jury service or activities dealing with certain emergencies or natural disasters. This leave is unpaid except for jury service.
7) Long service leave.
8) Public holidays and the entitlement to be paid for ordinary hours on those days.
9) Notice of termination and redundancy pay.
10) The right for new employees to receive the Fair Work Information Statement.

(The above NES standards were taken directly from the Fair Work Information Statement.)

This statement also elaborates on the following points:

- Right to request flexible working requirements
- Modern awards
- Agreement making
- Individual flexibility arrangements
- Freedom of association and workplace rights (general protections)
- Termination of employment
- Right of entry
- The Fair Work Ombudsman and the Fair Work Commission

For further clarification on the above points, this statement is available for a free in PDF download at www.fairwork.gov.au.

Letter of Offer with an Attached Job Description

When you are offered a job, you will receive a letter of offer or engagement. This is a contract made between you as the employee and the employer. It sets out the conditions of employment as well as your entitlements and remuneration. Template letters of offer for casual and full-time employees are available on the ombudsman website http://www.fairwork.gov.au/about-us/policies-and-guides/templates

At the end of an employment contract, there should be an attached job description. Signing the contract shows your acceptance of your job responsibilities, title, and associated KPIs. Violating this contract or not meeting establishing targets outlined in a job description (JD) serve as a justified for terminating employment. This is why understanding your job description is vital before signing a letter of engagement.

Here is a brief example of an attached JD:

Job Description	
01. Organisation Unit HR	**Cost Centre**
02. Job Title HR coordinator	**Name of Holder** Melissa Plume
03. Immediately Superior Unit HR manager	**Holder gets technical instructions from** Managing director/HR manager
04. Immediately subordinate dept./staff	**Holder gives technical instructions to** Administration and project supervisors
0.6 Powers/Authority Administration and project personnel; operates with some level of independence and is self-regulated in the sense that they determine their day-to-day priorities.	

0.7. Contacts	
07.1 Internal Maintaining communications with internal stakeholders, HR team and HR managers; liaising with employees to resolve issues and improve policies and procedures.	**07.2 External** Dealing confidently and professionally with potential candidates and members of the public who are seeking information from senior executives.

08. Education, experience, skills required for the position	
Diploma in human resources or an equivalent tertiary qualification. A minimum of four years HR generalist experience. Relevant understanding of HR strategy and methodology. Strong computer literacy skills, including a high level of proficiency with Word and Excel. Exceptional verbal and written communication skills. Strong organisational skills, the ability to successfully complete. several tasks concurrently, maintain high levels of attention to detail, maintain documentation and recordkeeping, and meet deadlines. Able to work collaboratively with the HR manager and the HR team.	

09. Main duties	**KPIs**
Assisting the hiring manager with talent development, retention and acquisition, and succession planning. Provide timely and accurate advice on policies, practises, recruitment, induction, and WH&S activities.	Submit monthly reports for turnover, L&D participation, remuneration, and employee performance. Meet all recruitment and selection deadlines and quotas.

| Maintain and update employee e-learning modules. Manage the recruitment and selection process in accordance with targeted selection methodology. | |

10. Work Health and Safety

Employees have a responsibility to take care to protect their own health and safety, and avoid adversely affecting the health and safety of others. Every employee has the following responsibilities:

Report and incident or hazards at work to the management of a direct supervisor.

Carry out all duties as detailed in the relevant health and safety procedures.

Obey any reasonable instruction aimed at protecting your health and safety while at work.

Use any equipment provided to protect your health and safety while at work.

Assist in the identification of hazards, the assessment of risks and the implementation of risk control measures.

Consider and provide feedback on any matters which may affect health and safety.

Adhere to the signed Drug and Alcohol Policy provided in your induction.

11. Positions held/functions performed on committees, institutions, commissions, etc.

Signatures	
Holder	**HR Personnel**
Name: Melissa Plume Signature:	Name: Natasha Spike Signature:

How to Ask for More Money

Consider this conversation in a performance review:

> Manager: "Why do you believe you deserve a pay rise?"

> Employee: "Because I do. I work harder than anyone else here."

No pay rise was given.

This is the one thing a lot of us dread. You've been in a job for a while, and everything is going great. You are hitting or exceeding your targets and have taken on more responsibilities, so you feel you should be getting paid more. So what do you do about it?

A lot of people just accept the fact that their pay rate is their pay rate. This could be out of a fear that asking for more pay could lead to losing the job or a fear of being seen as greedy. This is bad thinking. If you are taking on more responsibilities and are a very productive employee, you are entitled to more pay (within limits), and it is in the best interest of your employer to consider your request seriously and fairly.

Valid point, is it not? Of course it is! Although you have a valid case for a pay rise or even promotion, getting what you want can be solely dependent upon your delivery—upon how you ask for a pay rise. The most appropriate time to present your case is during a performance review, as you have been allocated a time one on one with a supervisor or manager during which you are encouraged to discuss your performance. You can highlight your achievements and contributions towards the organisation and communicate how you believe this entitles you to a higher pay scale.

Easier said than done!

When you're up for a review or appraisal, you are given notice. Use this time to prepare how you will present your case logically, using examples. You must be as objective as possible in your delivery. Avoid using your emotions as a basis or comparing yourself to other employees within your team or division. Your performance should speak for itself; comparing yourself to others only makes you seem as though you cannot justify your reasons.

Consider these circumstances: Melvin is facing his first three-month performance appraisal with his manager, Fadi. Melvin is a project coordinator and had been in a similar position only one year previously at another company. He feels that, although he has performed well, overall he hasn't performed exceptionally well—he secured only one large project in his three months. Despite this, his role has expanded beyond what was advertised. Melvin supports HR functioning and also delegates project tasks amongst other team members when Fadi is not present. He believes that he deserves a pay rise.

Note: You should monitor your performance consistently so you can be reassured that you have a solid performance record. Most employees and managers alike can recollect only the last couple of weeks of performance, which can bias a performance and pay review.

Case points in favour of a pay rise:

- Melvin's major accomplishment during his three months is proposing and securing a large deal for his company.
- His job responsibilities have increased, demonstrating his competencies in multitasking and communicating with other departments.
- Melvin assumes senior responsibilities in the absence of his manager and regularly delegates tasks to other team members without instruction.

Case points against a pay rise:

- Melvin secured only one deal, which is below the average rate for a project coordinator.
- He is still learning and undertaking training and development programs.

- He is a junior under the supervision of his manager.

By using these points, Melvin can demonstrate his value as an employee to his employer. He can conduct market research to find out the average salary package and determine whether his is at the low, middle, or high end of the range. This can give him leverage in his discussion when coupled with his value arguments.

Delivery of the case:

- Melvin provides a track record of his accomplishments and a list of responsibilities he has undertaken since he began employment.
- He presents market research regarding the average hourly rate of employees in similar positions with the relevant qualifications and work experience. He then contrasts this to his own pay package.
- He does not mention other employees in similar positions or departments but solely focuses on his own performance and potential to contribute to the organisation's growth.

Result: Pay rise provided.

Melvin presented his case in a logical and coherent order and support it with current market research. He remained unemotional and communicated his desire for recognition of his previous work and expanded job role. Fadi was receptive to this approach and was able to process the information fairly. This is the most effective approach to having a pay-rise request approved.

What If I Get Turned Down?

If your request for more money is denied, ask your manager what targets or performance improvements must be reached to be considered for a pay rise. This demonstrates your determination to take an active approach to further developing your skills for you and the organisation.

If your manager highlights any aspects of your performance which is lacking, ask if it is possible to reschedule a review in a couple of months when you have had sufficient opportunity to rectify your performance.

How Do I Ask for a Pay Rise Outside of a Performance Appraisal or Pay Review?

The strategy you use is the same as during a performance appraisal or pay review. It must be objective—supported by current market research—and highlight your contributions and performance over a period of time.

The difference lies in the timing. You have arranged with your manager to have a meeting outside the schedule of pay reviews or performance appraisals. Therefore, you must be prepared and sensitive to when this meeting occurs. For example, you should not expect to be granted a pay rise if the company has just recently downsized or is rapidly making budget cuts to cover losses. Expecting a pay rise in a struggling company is foolish. You must be aware of your organisation's capacity to provide the increase you desire. If it can't, it is not wise to schedule a meeting.

If you believe your organisation does have the capacity to grant you a pay rise, schedule the meeting soon after you've made a notable contribution to the organisation. This contribution will be at the forefront of your manager's mind, overriding previous performance hills. This will sway his or her decision in your benefit. You should also schedule a meeting when you've had a solid performance record with little or no blemishes. This gives your manager little ammunition to counteract your claim.

The delivery should be just as structured as Melvin's and well revised. Do not forget that your delivery is key!

Something to Be Wary of

A lot of people do not realise that internal recruiters as well as external recruiters have quotas to fill. Internal recruiters have certain targets: the amount of people they must hire within a certain time frame to satisfy their KPIs. In saying this, although you're sitting for a role and you know that you're being offered a job or hired internally, do not think that the HR team or recruitment specialists have what's best for you or the organisation in mind.

Also be wary that internal recruiters will try to sell you the job. They will mention all the positive aspects and ignore the negative ones. This can give you unrealistic job expectations. You do not want to be one of those people who accept a letter of offer and two weeks later realise that it is not the job they signed up for or the organisation they thought it was.

Avoiding this type of deception is difficult, but you can take some steps to prevent this. Once you've been offered the position, tell them that you're excited about the opportunity, but to ensure that the job and organisation are for you, ask to be a "fly on wall" for a few hours. In other words, ask if it's possible to observe someone in the same or a similar role before you accept. If they are not willing to grant this request, perhaps it's because the internal recruiters have deceived you. Be wary!

Knowing Your Work Entitlements

Annual Leave Entitlements

This differs for full-time, part-time, and casual employees, subcontractors, and shift workers. The information below is generic and can change slightly according to an organisation's HR policy and the industry you work in.

Paid annual leave is available to the following employees:

- Full-time employees are entitled to accrue 140 hours (four weeks) of annual leave per year of continuous service.
- Part-time staff members accrue annual leave on a proportionate basis of the full-time entitlement.
- Annual leave does not accrue during unpaid periods of leave. Public holidays are not deducted from annual leave.

Employees who are ill while on annual leave may apply for their annual leave to be recredited for the period of illness, provided they submit a medical certificate covering the period of annual leave. Employees can also submit a statutory declaration, provided they have accrued enough carers and sick leave. This will then be deducted from the employee's personal/carers leave entitlements.

Payment

Payment is the employee's hourly rate they would normally be paid had they been working. Payment in lieu of untaken annual leave will be made to staff members on termination of employment or to the estate of the deceased staff member in case of death.

Taking Annual Leave

- Submission of annual leave by an employee must be a minimum of four weeks prior to the anticipate leave date.
- Approval of annual leave will be at the discretion of the organisation who will consider (1) the organisation's operational requirements and (2) the personal circumstances of the employee.

Employees should aim to take their annual leave within twelve months of it being credited or accrued. The organisation's payroll department will advise a minimum of four weeks notice if an employee is required to take annual leave. If annual leave is denied, the organisation will then negotiate an alternative period of annual leave suitable to the entitled employee.

Leave in Advance

If during the first year of employment an employee has not accrued sufficient annual leave, he or she may, with authorisation, take annual leave without pay, or up to five days' paid leave in advance.

Cashing Out Annual Leave

Subject to legislation, employees may be able to cash out their annual leave. Only in exceptional circumstances would an organisation allow this.

Leaving an Organisation

When leaving an organisation, employees will be paid any accrued annual leave at their base rate of pay for ordinary hours. Any negative annual leave balance on termination of employment will be adjusted to a credit taken from termination pay.

National Employment Standards (NES)

The Fair Work Act 2009 established ten minimum conditions every employee, regardless of what industry or modern award they are covered by, is entitled to:

- Maximum working hours per week are thirty-eight hours. The employer can request reasonable additional hours.
- Requests can be made for flexible working arrangements.
- Parental leave: employees with twelve months continuous service have twelve months unpaid parental leave for birth/adoption.
- Annual leave: employees (other than casuals) are entitled to four weeks of paid annual leave [five weeks of shift work]. They may be able to cash out annual leave.
- Personal/carer leave: employees (other than casuals) have ten days of personal/carer's leave and two days of compassionate leave.
- Community service leave: paid leave for jury service and unpaid leave for recognised community activities.
- Long-service leave.
- Public holiday work.
- Notice of termination/redundancy: the employer must give the employee written notice of the day of termination, and the employee is entitled to redundancy pay as set out in the legislation.

A Fair Work Information Statement, published by the Fair Work Ombudsman, must be given to all new employees on induction.

Small Business Unfair Dismissal

The Fair Work Ombudsman outlines a code for small business employers to follow. The employee must be warned verbally, or preferably in writing, that he or she risks being dismissed if there is no improvement. The employer must provide the employee with an opportunity to respond to the warning and give a reasonable chance to rectify the problem. Rectifying the problem might involve the employer providing additional training and ensuring the employee knows the employer's job expectations.

A small business employer will be required to provide evidence of compliance with the code if the employee makes a claim for unfair dismissal to Fair Work Australia, including evidence that a warning has been given. Evidence may include a completed checklist, copies of written warnings, and a statement of termination or signed witness statements.

If dismissal is deemed harsh, unreasonable, not consistent with the small business code, or not a genuine case of redundancy, employees are protected as long as they have satisfied a probationary period of employment (six to twelve months) and are covered by an award or agreement.

It is the responsibility of the HR manager to defend unfair dismissal claims.

Superannuation

The minimum amount of superannuation payment required by employers is regulated by Australian legislation. The minimum can change annually or when the legislation is reviewed. It is the responsibility of HR departments to monitor these changes. However, small organisations can be misinformed about this minimum. Employees should take it upon themselves to make sure they are paid the minimum super and that these superannuation instalments are evident on payslips.

If you're unsure about your working entitlements, visit http://www.fairwork.gov.au/pages/default.aspx. The ombudsman website provides information on the Fair Work Act 2009 and the National Employment

Standards, which employers must abide by. You can download a PDF version of the National Employment Standards Information Statement directly from their website.

Understanding Worker Health and Safety (WH&S)

Legislation clearly states that WH&S is everyone's responsibility. We all have a duty to ensure that everything "reasonably practicable" is done to protect the health and safety of people in the workplace.

What Are My WH&S Responsibilities?

Each worker has an obligation to do the following:

- Comply with safe work practises, with the intent of avoiding injury to themselves and others.
- Take reasonable care of the health and safety of themselves and others.
- Comply with any direction given by management for health and safety.
- Not misuse or interfere with anything provided for health and safety.
- Report any potential hazards in the workplace to your manager or supervisor.
- Record all injuries in the WH&S Injury Booklet and note immediate action taken.

What Are My Rights As an Employee?

- You have the right to a safe and healthy workplace.
- You have the right to information, training, and supervision so you can carry out your health and safety obligations.

Setting Up Your Workstation Ergonomically

An ergonomic workstation maintains a healthy body posture. Below are elements of a workstation with a desktop computer.

- Gaze slightly down
- Shoulders relaxed
- Elbows at ninety degrees
- Hips at ninety degrees or greater
- Feet flat on the floor

Following are tips for arranging your computer workstation:

- Make sure you sit facing the screen.
- Place your computer at about arm's length from your position in the chair.
- Ensure the keyboard is close enough to you so you do not have to stretch to type.
- Adjust the height of your monitor so that your eyes fall about two to three inches below the top of the monitor.
- Adjust your chair so that your elbows are at about ninety degrees.
- Tilt your keyboard slightly away from you so that your wrists are straight.
- When typing from a document, place the document as close to the computer as possible.
- Arrange commonly used items close to your body.
- Take a break. Stretch, walk around, and rest your eyes at least every hour.
- Avoid having a window behind you. The light will affect the screen's contrast, making it difficult to read what is on the screen.

Job and Employment Scams

Job scams are designed to target those who are searching for a job or a job change. These scams state that they can provide a lot of money for little work, with flexible working arrangements and/or working from home.

These con artists often post convincing advertisements on the web and on well-known job-seeking sites. Do not ever send your signature!

Work-from-Home Scams

Work-from-home scams often promise flexible working hours, little work, and some form of data-entry position. They target stay-at-home mothers and those looking for extra cash. These can include money-laundering schemes or requiring an initial payment, such as to purchase a "starter kit."

These scams are advertised on job boards, public noticeboards, and through spam emails. Protect yourself by immediately deleting spam emails and not giving your personal details to unreputable sources—that is, those without a website, ABN, or physical address listed in online directories.

Guaranteed Employment and Income Scams

A lot of scammers send a spam email, followed by a call offering a job. These offers usually require a payment for a "business plan," materials, or software. They may also ask you to make goods which will never be sold, as they will not be of high quality. The software provided will also not function as promised.

Superannuation Scams

These scams are designed to target those approaching retirement. They promise to "unlock" your superannuation early at the cost of a small fee. In Australia, you are unable to have access to your superannuation unless you can prove you are facing financial hardship or make a case based on "compassionate" grounds. Anyone who offers it to you earlier is a con artist.

It is important to know about this particular scam, especially if you are facing financial hardship due to unemployment. Do not engage the services of those who promote under the pretence of being financial advisers. If you believe you are suffering financial hardship, contact your superannuation provider. Ask for a "financial hardship" package, and fill out the forms.

The way scammers make their money is by deceiving your superannuation fund holder, once you provide them with your membership and personal details. Your superannuation fund will accidentally pay the "financial adviser" portions of your super. Once this happens, you've lost your money.

Money Transfer Scams

These are often money-laundering "jobs" which can lead to you being prosecuted for your unintentional involvement. They can also be simply a means of gaining your bank account details so they can steal your money. Common sense should prevail when trying to discern if something is a scam.

Example 1

Very urgent,

I want you to help me transfer the sum of US$12.5Million dollars into your account in your country.

This money belongs to my late client, who died in a car accident few years ago with his family leaving nobody for the claim. As his personal lawyer, the bank has written the last warning letter to me, to present his next of kin or have the account blocked and the money confiscated. This transaction is legal and risk free You will get 40%, 50% for me and 10% will be for expenses.

Please my dear if you are interested to assist in this claim, then get back to me through my private email with your full personal date's listed bellow to enable immediate commencement of the transfer proceedings.

Your Full Name … … … … … … … … …

Occupation … … … … … … … … … … … … … …

Age ... ...

Maritals Startus ... ...

Country ... ...

Home or Office Address ... ...

Privatetelephonenumber... ... ...

Private email.address ... ...

As soon as i receive all your daters i will then give you more details and how to proceed and get the fund into your account immediately.

Waiting to hearing from you as soon as possible.

Best Regard,
Barrister Uba Eric.(esq

As you will notice, these email have numerous grammatical and spelling errors, as they have been written by a foreigner. This a key hint in detecting scams.

Example 2

Hello my dear,

I am Madam Jethren Corsy from Sierra-Leone married to Mr. Williams Corsy, he was dealing on Gold and Diamond, who died of cancer leaving me and my only son Ken who is 7 years now, and before his death he deposited US$10.5 Million in one of the reputable banks which I will disclose to you once I receive your reply.

Since the death of my husband, his brothers have been seriously chasing me around with constant threats, trying to suppress me so that they might have the documents of his landed properties and confiscate them. They have successfully collected all his properties, yet they never stopped there, they told me to surrender all bank accounts of my late husband, which I did, but I never disclose to them of this deposit. Because my husband made the deposit in a suspense fixed account with a clause attached to it for onward transfer into a foreign account.

Now that the situation is becoming uncontrollable because of pressure on me from the family members, which I will no longer like to take more risk staying here with my only son who is just Seven year old, I am now soliciting for your help to stand as my foreign business partner to receive the fund into your account. You will help me to invest the money into real estate once I come over there with my son.

So if you accept to be my partner to receive the fund in your account, get back to me for more details. Please call me after reading: +22998520796

Thanks,
Madam Jethren Corsy

This email targets your empathy and that of those who are always willing to help others, even if they do not know them. This is very unfortunate!

Example 3

From: Lotus Bank- Australia's No1 Bank[mailto:efileteam. support@soft.com]

Sent: Friday, 21 February 2014 6:36 AM

To: melo.hulme@gmail.com

Subject: Account vulnerable, temporarily locked melo. hulme@gmail.com

Dear melo.hulme@gmail.com,

Recently, Lotus Bank has implemented several new security measures that will block all unauthorised access to your account.

Due to several security scans on Thursday, February 21, 2014 at 4:24:51 AM AEDT, we discovered some suspicious connection attempts in your connection history.

Therefore your account has been automatically marked as vulnerable and has been temporarily locked.

To regain access to the account and use our online services, please follow these requirements:

-> Go to: https://security.lotus.com.au/user_updates/AccountSecurity/

-> Allow up to 4 hours to update your account.

This application filters all connections through a secure connection, so all data is transmitted securely, and also blocks your IP address if there are any suspicious fields.

This will prevent unauthorised access to your account.

This notification aims to prevent and protect you from losing any information and make your online bussiness more safe.

Rose McRamon,

Lotus Bank Security Center,

Thursday, February 21, 2014

E-Mail ID: GRU_3206782096KR

This email makes "Lotus Bank" customers believe that their account security has been jeopardised. By following the link, they provide the scammers their account number and login details.

Employer Scams

These scammers target employers using free job boards to display advertisements. They make employers or HR personnel believe that their advertisements have been removed and that their accounts need verification. A link is included in the body of the email, which leads to a website. This website mimics the real job board, but the link will be different and have references to the real domain.

The website which opens will require your login details. From there you will be redirected to credit card details. It will state that you will not be charged or that no fees will be incurred for account verification. This is how they trick people! You will know this is definitely a scam as your advertisements will still be posted. Be wary, as scams occur with very reputable job boards and employer websites. Here is an example:

From: Gulian [mailto:noreply@gulian.com.au]

Sent: Thursday, 20 March 2014 10:10 AM

To: careers@melohum.com.au

Subject: Your ad has been flagged for removal

Dear Gulian User,

Thanks for your Ad however we're afraid that your Ad has been removed because it was flagged as fraud.

We need you to confirm your identity. Please follow this link:

Confirm Account Identity

For more information, please review our posting policies. Any future Ads will also be removed until your account will be verified.

Thanks
The Gulian Team

Phishing

The term *phishing* is used to describe scams which try to elicit personal, bank account, or credit cards details from targets under the pretence of a financial institution and/or legitimate businesses based in Australia. They construct emails using signatures including real business logos, formats, and email addresses which mimic their domain names. For example, they might use www.nab.com.au/login/bix as a domain, which is similar to NAB's domain name.

If you're unsure about the source of an email or call, do not give out your information over the phone or via an email. Visit your institution if the nature of the issue is urgent.

Identity Theft

When you submit your application for a job, a lot of people do not realise how much unnecessary information they have included in their CV. Some include their full name, full address, mobile number, email, and date of birth. All these are big no-nos! Why? It's simple. You've just provided scammers with enough information to steal your identity.

Clever scammers are now replicating popular or reputable job board websites to gather this type of information. They use similar links to the real domain names and ask you to submit your CV. Some will even go as far as providing you a letter of offer (for jobs based at home) and asking you to sign and send a scanned copy … now they have your signature!

Be vigilant when it comes to giving out your personal information. Begin by limiting information you provide on your CV, as employers do not need to know exactly where you live or your age until you're offered the job.

You might think that no one steals your identity without a copy of your birth certificate or other identification. Some loan companies or credit card companies are lax in their credit checks or the amount of information needed to open an account. It is quite easy for a scammer to use this information to open credit cards and create a debt in your name.

This chapter is written only to make you aware of the identity theft possibilities so that you eliminate unnecessary information from your CV. Be cautious!

If I believe my identity has been stolen, what do I do?

The following steps are actions you can take in the case your identity has been stolen. These steps are only suggestions; RCI Success will not take responsibility for any consequences you experience as a result of following this guidance.

1. Call your banking institution and increase the security on your accounts. Additional questions beyond the standard security questions, such as "What is your date of birth, full address, full name, and email address?" should be made. It should not be a question which can be gathered from your birth certificate, such as "What is your mother's maiden name?" The questions and answers should be something only you can know and answer.

2. If necessary, cancel your current credit cards and instruct your bank that you will not be taking out any loans or opening any new accounts. Make them completely aware that your identity has been stolen.

3. Cancel your current driver's license and quickly reissue a new one. To reissue, you must bring a witness who has known you for at least two years, original copies of your birth certificate, a Medicare card, and other forms of identification. Once you fill out the forms and your witness has signed, the RTA will take a lovely picture, and you will have a new license number and card. A new card prevents thieves using your old license number to steal your identity. Although there is a small fee involved, it can save you a lot of hassles with loan and credit card debts.

4. The most important step is reporting your identity theft to the federal police. They treat this type of crime as a serious offence. Visit www.afp.gov.au for further information.

Summary

Scamming and identity theft are illegal and can get you into trouble with the government. Don't lose hope. Use the guidance provided by this book to find legal and stable employment in Australia.

If you require further information regarding the scams above, visit www.scamwatch.gov.au or contact the Australian Competition and Consumer Commission.

Your Rights to Work in Australia

Towards the end of a one-hour session with a client, I asked what type of visa she was on. She replied, "A student visa." I was astounded that she said this so calmly. She had just finished her master's degree and was planning on finding work in Australia and staying for the rest of her life. How could she do this if she wasn't sponsored, wasn't a permanent resident, and hadn't gotten a working visa? The answer is, she couldn't. If she didn't find employment before her student visa expired, she would be deported to her home country.

I immediately advised that she apply for a working visa before continuing her search or, if she didn't want to wait, to include her visa status on her CV as a minimum. The message of this story is that if you are an international student or have immigrated and are seeking Australian employment, be aware of your working rights and the type of visa you need. Also inform potential employers of your visa status, as not informing them is viewed as deceitful.

Here is a brief outline of some of the Australian working restrictions attached to visas.

Working Holiday Visa

The working holiday visa is granted to those who desire to work and holiday in Australia for up to one year. It allows you to stay in Australia and work up to six months with one employer and study for a maximum of four months. If you're already in Australia and wish to stay in Australia, you must apply for a second Working Holiday Visa before your first expires.

There are certain criteria you need to satisfy in order for your second working holiday visa to be provided. This chapter of the book focuses only on the working requirements. You must have already completed three months of specified work in regional Australia. This work must have already been completed on your first Working Holiday Visa. Only specific industries are approved for this regional work. For further details, visit www.immi.gov.au.

A visa holder, you need to keep evidence of employment while in Australia, such as

- payslips;
- tax returns;
- group certificates;
- employer references; and
- original bank statements.

If you are granted a second Working Holiday Visa, you are able to stay in Australia for up to twenty-four months.

Student Visa

If you have been granted permission to work while on your student visa, there will be certain working restrictions. You can begin work in Australia only once your studies have begun. You are then permitted to work a maximum of forty hours per fortnight during each study session. Once a session has ended, you can work an unlimited amount of hours.

Before you begin applying for jobs, understand your Australian working rights. It would be a shame if you accepted a job only to realise that you cannot legally work.

Chapter 7

The Recruitment and Selection Process

When an organisation makes the decision to fill a position or open a vacancy, it undergoes the following three steps:

1) Develop a position description and associated KPIs.
2) Develop a job advertisement to source suitable candidates.
3) Undergo filtering and selection processes.

You have already begun to understand these processes by knowing in-depth what practical steps human resource personnel and recruitment consultants undergo. However, there is a lot of work occurring behind the scenes which is not revealed to candidates. This chapter will enlighten you to these processes.

If an organisation has instigated HR policies and procedures which uphold Equal Employment Opportunity (EEO) standards, their recruitment and selection procedures are aimed at being systematic and consistent. They also aim to attract, select, and retain the most competitive and high-quality pool of candidates possible.

Equal Employment Opportunity standards are based on equity. The principles of equity are based on a commitment to following procedures, which avoid all direct and indirect forms of discrimination. Antidiscrimination laws and regulations in Australia are very explicit on what cannot be used to determine a person's suitability to a role:

Gender	Age
Pregnancy	Ethnicity
Marital Status	Religion
Parental Status	Political beliefs
Sexual orientation	Association with or relation to someone with an identified attribute listed above

If you feel as though you have been discriminated against in a recruitment and selection process based on one or more of the above attributes, contact the ombudsman body.

Step 1: Design a Position Description

The job description must be as detailed as possible. This could be difficult if the position is new. Job descriptions should include a duty statement, the main job objectives, and the titles associated with this or these objectives. Clear KPIs should be outlined in a table with measurable outcomes. By organising a job description, writing an accurate job advertisement has just become easier.

Before a job advertisement is released, the selection criteria used to distinguish between high-quality and uncompetitive candidates must first be established. This criteria is used for shortlisting candidates, ranking candidates based on their interview performance, and conducting reference checks. The selection criteria can encompass a variety of factors including:

- qualifications,
- previous work experience,
- knowledge and skills, and
- personal attributes.

Within each of these areas, essential criteria must first be outlined. This can then be followed by desirable but not necessary selection criteria. This allows a wide variety of candidates to apply and reduces application discouragement by high and rigid standards. This also grants organisation representatives the flexibility and discretion to filter through a larger pool and thereby choose a suitable candidate.

Highly experienced human-resource personnel will be able to decipher a person's work experience and thereby extract associated knowledge and skills. They will also take into account the capacities of candidates to acquire and develop new skills and knowledge.

Step 2: Draft and Release a Job Advertisement

The aim of a job advertisement is to cast a net which catches a wide variety of candidates who could potentially fill the vacancy. These advertisements can be either internal or external. Which type of route an organisation takes is in line with the position's requirements. For instance, vacancies can be advertised internally if the position is similar to other roles within the organisation and there are multiple departments where the opportunity for a transfer or career progression is possible. External recruitment can be used when new ideas are a priority for the organisation, or it is not within the organisation's capacity to employ one of their own into a different role.

By advertising internally and externally, HR personnel need to weigh the pros and cons of each pathway.

Internal vs. External Recruiting

Internal Recruiting	
Pros: Increase morale of employees knowing there are career progression opportunities. Easier to assess an applicant's suitability with internal work records available. High performance is rewarded. Less costs involved in attracting a high quality pool of candidates.	Cons: Risk of "idea cloning." Disappointment among those not appointed to the new position. An appraisal system and procedure must be implemented. Little diversification of ideas and old culture retained.

External Recruiting	
Pros:	Cons:
New ideas and expertise brought into the organisation. No claims of favourtism can be made as internal promotion was not used. Aligns with EEO standards and Affirmative Action strategies. Can be used to change an organisational culture rapidly. Diversifies a workforce.	New recruit may not fit with organisational culture. Training and development may be required, especially with company systems and software. Evaluating a candidate's past work history is more difficult and requires more steps in the selection process.

Creating an Advertisement

So an organisation has decided what is the most efficient mode of advertisement. A draft is then written. This is the end result of step 2. Highly experienced HR personnel draft advertisements which capture high-quality candidates' attention. This is most commonly executed using the AIDA technique.

AIDA is an acronym for Attention, Interest, Desire, and Action. It organises an advertisement into sections, providing cohesion and avoiding large clumps of information, which are unattractive to the eye.

- *Attention:* Attention is gained through the job title. This title is usually not too specific to an organisation, such as "Level 5 Administration." It avoids jargon and is generic so that candidates from a range of industries understand the type of job and the requirements expected.
- *Interest:* This section of the advertisement focuses on the opportunity the role represents and the attached responsibilities. Interest is garnered by highlighting attractive features of the position, peripheral benefits, and what it is like to work for the organisation. Human resources personnel write from the perspective of potential employees. What would they be interested

in? Would what I have written make me want to apply if I was seeking a similar role?

- This section incorporates the responsibilities, what is expected of successful applicants, and career progression and developmental opportunities.
- *Desire:* Desire targets the core reason why people work: to earn money. While stating remuneration packages and perks, the ideal type of person is also mentioned. This could include attributes such as a friendly and outgoing demeanour, or a list of soft skill criterion: excellent verbal and written communication skills, attention to detail, etc.
- *Action:* This is where HR personnel or recruitment consultants want you to apply. After you read their sales pitch, they need to finally convince you that this is the job for you. They include a call to action prompting the reader to submit necessary documentation.

Hopefully, you can now appreciate the hard work which goes into developing a job description and vacancy announcement. Writing efficient job advertisements is not easy. You can also look at a job position with a questioning eye: What aspects of the job role are they neglecting to tell me? Why have they listed only responsibilities? Is this an organisation with a high turnover rate?

Step 3: Filtering through Applications and Creating Shortlists

This process is quite long and monotonous for HR personnel, especially when they've just posted an advertisement on SEEK and within two hours they already have two hundred CVs sitting in your inbox. Yes, that's right! You're not the only one out there fighting for a job. HR staff are usually overwhelmed by the responses they receive. When they are genuine and kind people, the task of rejecting and judging people based off their CVs and cover letters can be difficult. Some struggle to deal with this part of their job description, but it has to be done. So when you're dealing with HR personnel, you need to understand that a lot of them do not take pleasure in rejecting candidates and, in a sense, determining their fate. Take this insider perspective and use it to try to understand the processes.

The recruitment and selection steps involved include the following:

- receiving applications,
- acknowledging applicants via telephone or via an email,
- reviewing applicants and beginning the filtering process,
- nominating staff members responsible for the recruitment and selection process and
- constructing a shortlist from candidate applications.

Receiving Job Applications

When a company advertises externally on job boards or websites such as SEEK, the HR personnel nominate one or two email accounts to where applications are directed. This is usually a careers or job-specific email not known to the public unless included at the bottom of an advertisement. Small to medium businesses might include a personalised email address. Recruitment consultants responsible for handling their clients' needs often include their work email address so that all enquiries are directed to them.

To save time and so that people do not hassle HR personnel, an automated email is often sent to candidates when their applications have been received. This puts the applicants at peace, knowing that their application was received, and it prevents HR personnel receiving duplicates and being harassed.

Filtering Applications

This is a very long process. With hundreds of CVs being deposited into their inbox, HR personnel can spend only an allocated amount of time reading them. This is why your CV and cover letter have to be neat, structured, and easy to absorb, with information relevant to the position.

Creating a Shortlist

Once personnel have sifted through all or the first portion of candidates, they likely have developed a shortlist. These are the "good" of the bunch—the candidates to be contacted over the phone. This shortlist is not final but constantly changes during the recruitment process. For instance, an HR staff member contacts candidate A on their shortlist, and after speaking with her, he has gathered that she is not enthusiastic about the role and not as experienced as represented on her CV. Candidate A is then removed from the shortlist. This happens also with candidates B, C, and D. The shortlist has now been cut in half. He then goes through his pool of applications and reselects other "good" candidates.

So, if you receive a telephone call, and the organisation's representative states that he will shortlist you, this does not mean that you will then be interviewed. If he contacts other candidates which are more qualified and performed better on the telephone, your shortlist position can be taken. Keep this in mind: shortlisting does not equal an interview.

Selecting Applicants for an Interview

If there is a team of personnel working together for recruitment and selection, this is when they meet and discuss shortlisted applications. After discussing the results on initial contact, the team decides which candidates will be contacted for an interview.

When an individual is responsible for recruitment and selection, you can tell. She is the one you will always lease with if you have questions. You will also know whether your telephone performance was adequate, as she will schedule an interview instantly. Note that HR personnel have little time and many duties to complete to find the right candidate. Therefore you need to make time for the interview, even if the suggested times are inconvenient. If you're not seen as being flexible, they will find someone else. Recruitment consultants especially are pushed for time and are extremely busy people.

Notifying Unsuccessful Shortlisted Applicants

A generic email is usually sent to all those who have applied once a candidate has been placed and the recruitment and selection process finalised. This likely states that the email recipient was unsuccessful and wishes him or her all the best in the future. Others might say they are keeping the candidate's records on file; he or she may be highly skilled and suited to another job rather than the one applied to.

Human resources personnel must ask for permission first before storing any candidate's personal information. Most organisations see this as a common courtesy but also expect some backlash from desperate or eager candidates.

Step 4: Selection

It is the current belief amongst HR professionals that the more objective and structured the selection process, the greater the selection outcome. From this you can gather that selection processes within large corporations follow strict and consistent procedures when you are interviewed or engage with their HR personnel. They also use consistency to avoid discrimination and promote their organisation as an Equal Employment Opportunity employer.

The steps in the selection process can be summarised as the following:

- Arranging selection interviews
- Selection interviews
- Conducting reference checks
- Conducting other necessary checks
- Making a selection decision

Notice how much time and effort is designated for developing and following structured and fair recruitment and selection procedures. Acknowledging this hard work should deter candidates from being angry at HR personnel who "take forever" to get back to them or do not return phone calls. In some cases, yes, they are being rude. Or you did not make their shortlist, and they plan on informing you via a generic email. However, in some cases, the HR personnel are genuinely busy and can designate only a certain amount of time to liaising with candidates—shortlisted or not shortlisted.

Arranging Selection Interviews

Quite often HR personnel work in small teams focused on filling one or multiple positions. As a team, they also have quotas to satisfy which are part of their individual job KPIs. This means HR personnel need to fill a specific amount of positions per week to meet their quota or team target. With these KPIs, HR personnel can take two different approaches:

- *Approach A:* They can try to fill positions as quickly as possible to satisfy their KPIs, disregarding suitability and whether the candidate would be competent and satisfied taking on the role.
- *Approach B:* HR personnel recognise that quality is better than quantity, and if they do not meet their quota it is only because they were seeking out the best candidates. Approach B acknowledges that filling a position with an incompetent or unenthusiastic candidate increases turnover rates whilst increasing quotas.

As a candidate, you would hope that you have dealings with approach B HR professionals. They take into consideration your desires for career progression and whether the organisation is a right fit for you. If you have dealings with approach A professionals, you need to be wary that they are using a sales pitch—telling you only the best bits of the job whilst providing unrealistic job expectations.

Selection Interview Conduct

Failure to find the right candidate is not always due to a poor pool of candidates, but to the HR personnel failing to conduct reliable and consistent interviews. Personnel may be unable to fairly and effectively discriminate between suitable and unsuitable candidates and thereby can't fill the vacancy. Interview reliability may be limited by the following selection interview conduct:

- Speaking too much and failing to elicit relevant and concise information from candidates
- No questions related directly to the job

- Not establishing appropriate and fair ways of assessing answers
- Framing questions which hint towards acceptable answers for some and not all candidates

So if you walk out of an interview feeling like you aced it and then find out later that you didn't make the cut, it may actually be due to the interviewer's incompetence. She did not allow you the correct platform to canvass your skills and knowledge, costing you the job. When this happens, it is a shame not only for you but also for the organisation the HR professional represents. Chances are that she will finalise the recruitment and selection process with a candidate unfit for the role or of a lower quality. This will then cost them money as they will need to find someone else as a replacement or to implement training and development to fill their skills and knowledge gaps.

Concluding an Interview

Personnel should provide the opportunity for candidates to ask questions. This allows them to speak without direction and lets them address any issues they have. It also gives them an indication of the most important aspect of the job for them. If they straight away ask about remuneration, HR personnel will assume that is their primary concern. If candidates ask about career progression and what it is like to work for the organisation, personnel will assume that this is important to them.

Efficient professionals then inform the interviewee when to expect to receive news about a decision. This is not only common courtesy but prevents being harassed. If the HR professional does not mention this at the interview conclusion, it is best to mention it. You do not want to be bothering him, as this could harm your chances, and he does not want to be bothered. So do both of you a favour and ask at the end of an interview.

Reference Checks

When personnel conduct reference checks, they try to validate the information provided by the candidate during the interview and on their

CV. It is the norm to conduct two reference checks over the telephone. During these checks, professionals follow these steps:

- Build rapport with the referee by asking about the work relationship between himself and the applicant.
- Ask the referee to elaborate on the applicant's role and what he believes is her greatest strengths and weaknesses.
- The questions asked would be consistent for each reference check for each candidate.
- Describe the position to be filled and ask how he believes the applicant would be suitable for the role.

In large corporations, candidates are entitled to retrieve the reference checks. If this option is available, I recommend utilising it. If you've gotten to the last stage multiple times and still have no job offer, it would be in your best interest to know if it is because your referees are misrepresenting you.

Selecting the Right Candidate

Once the team of HR personnel or the HR professional has made a selection decision, the unsuccessful applicants must be informed as soon as possible. This is done once a letter of offer has been accepted by the selected candidate.

Unsuccessful candidates are often informed that they have not progressed to various recruitment stages via an email. Here are several examples:

Example 1

> *Thank you for your recent application for the position of Administration Officer—12345.*
>
> *Due to the large number of applications received, reviewing them has taken considerable time. We apologise for the delay in communicating with you and any inconvenience caused.*

We have now completed the shortlisting stage of our recruitment process and advise that on this occasion you have been unsuccessful in progressing to the next stage of the process.

We thank you for your interest in this position and encourage you to apply for any other position that you are interested at Company X by visiting our jobs website http://jobs.companyX. com.au.

Example 2

We sincerely thank you for your application for the position of administration assistant (junior) with Company Y and appreciate the time you took to attend the interview.

We received a large number of applications with relevant qualifications for this role. Unfortunately, in this instance your application has been unsuccessful.

Thank you once again for your interest and time. We wish you every success in your future employment.

Example 3

We acknowledge receipt of your application and take this opportunity to thank you for your interest in employment at Company Z.

Our recruitment process is thorough, and selection of suitable candidates for interview should be completed within three weeks. If your application is to progress to the interview stage, we will be in direct contact with you to arrange a suitable time.

We would like to inform you that the information contained in your application will be confidentially maintained in accordance with the principles of the Privacy Act 1988.

*If we have not made contact with you within three weeks, we
thank you again for your interest in working with Company
Z and wish you well in your search for satisfying employment.*

If the chosen candidate does not accept the offer, a second round of
interviews is then conducted. Unsuccessful candidates are entitled to
feedback. You can access the records and ask personnel to justify their
decisions and on what grounds they chose someone else over you.

The notion that recruitment and selection processes are simplistic is an
insult to HR professionals and recruitment consultants alike. A lot of
effort and resources are devoted to finding the right people for specific
jobs. People are essentially "human resources" and serve as the life force
of an organisation. When a position is vacant, it is fundamental to find
the right person so that the candidate, the organisation, and the other
workers all benefit.

Chapter 8

An Employer's Perspective

Organisations genuinely do want to satisfy the needs of their employees by incorporating more opportunities for employee enrichment, job rotation, and job enlargement. However, these must be coupled with an increase in wage or salary if employees undertake greater responsibilities on a continual basis. Organisations also attempt to engage employees in cross-functional projects to break down a silo mentality—that is, artificial physical and psychological barriers to people mobility within the organisation. Although satisfying employees' needs can be a primary concern, recruitment and selection practises must benefit the company and be in alignment with the overall recruitment and selection goals and strategies.

Recruitment and selection methods chosen by an organisation depend on weighing the associated benefits and disadvantages of each method. Following are two of the methods.

E-Recruitment

- Lowers costs: costs devoted to traditional methods of recruitment such as newspapers, advertisements, and journal articles are avoided.
- Increased exposure: the Internet is able to reach a wider net of potential employees than traditional forms of advertising. For example, newspapers are seen only by locals, so applicants would be limited to the business's area.

- Speed: online advertisements are immediate, with no delays for printing. Responses are also instant.

If an organisation assesses its own limited ability to fulfil a job vacancy or find high-quality candidates, it engages the services of a recruitment agency. Advertisements are a part of recruitment agencies' services and thereby hide the identity of the hiring organisation. This provides benefits to the hiring organisation, but it also raises a debate about whether it is or is not ethical to identify an organisation's name on advertisements.

Hiding the identities of organisations can be viewed as unethical or disadvantageous in the following ways:

- Potential employees may have strong beliefs and political affiliations which will be contradicted by applying to specific positions in certain organisations. For example, a political activist against the unregulated draining of water table resources would be against applying for a position at a company which has received a lot of media attention regarding its water consumption.
- An organisation's name can help attract potential employees if it holds a good reputation and has been successfully branded to be an employer of choice. If its name is not displayed, its reputation is unknown and can be met with suspicion by applicants. Questions such as "Why would they not show their name? Is this organisation trustworthy?" can cause someone not to apply. Even if the organisation is not well known or a recognised employer of choice, displaying the organisation's name can help limit the number of applicants who would not be interested if they knew the nature of the industry and type of organisation.

For these reasons, it can be seen as wrong and disadvantageous not to display the hiring organisation's name in recruitment advertisements.

What Type of Recruiters Do Organisations Use?

As stated previously, an organisation ultimately makes its decision about the types of agencies and services that are outsourced by weighing the positives and negatives associated with each type of service.

Contingency Recruitment vs. Retained Recruitment

The table below outlines the factors which would influence an organisation to engage either contingency or retained recruitment services. The table serves as an elaboration upon HR and recruitment lingo discussed previously.

Contingency	Retained
Suitable for • Low-level/entry-level positions • A large pool of applicants • Filling many job vacancies • When speed is more important than high-quality candidates • Hiring manager wants control over filtering, acquiring, and selection process	Suitable for Senior/executive positions • Confidentiality is critical, and may involve headhunting • High-quality candidates are of great importance • Full working history of each applicant is required • Professional recruitment and selection assistance is required to fill job vacancies

How Long Do Recruitment and Selection Processes Take?

Contingency recruiting is very quick. With low-level job vacancies, there are usually multiple candidates suitable and available for the position. This makes it easier for recruitment consultants to present candidates to their clients. The retained process is more complex. It involves the following stages:

1. The consultant has a one-on-one meeting with the client to learn about the specific candidate requirements, the organisational culture, and the type of management style the candidate must be suited to.

2. The consultant uses job advertisements to target good candidates who have a stable working history. A long list of candidates is constructed.

3. Screening begins via consistent and structured telephone interviews.

4. Once interviewed, the most suitable candidates are presented to the client by sending their CVs and cover letters. The client then decides which candidates they would like to interview.

5. When the client chooses its top few, consultants conduct reference checks before or after the client meets with the candidate. The timing of checks is dependent on the client's discretion.

6. From this point forward, the consultant serves as a mediator in closing the deal between the client and the top candidate. Communication between the consultant and candidate continues for the first few months of employment to ensure her or she is comfortable and fitting into the organisation.

These multiple stages extend the time taken for a retained consultant to be paid the total fee, unlike a contingency consultant.

The Blame Game

Unfortunately, no matter what type of organisation you work for—whether it is large, small, or medium-sized—you will always face organisational politics—or the blame game. This game has the following parameters:

• Two or more parties have a confrontation.
• People in upper management or executive positions blame wrongdoings, poor performance, or project outcomes on employees.

- "He says, she says" become an issue; employees' verbal communication and actions are in contradiction, and a mutual understanding on the company's direction is not found.

For most people, this is the norm in their work experience, and they do not realise the harmful effects of the game. The blame game can do the following:

- Threaten your job security
- Cause you a lot of stress
- Develop or maintain a toxic working environment and culture

For these reasons, you need to develop strategies to reduce your vulnerability to litigation and to protect your job security.

So, have you played the game? If you are new to the workforce, it is likely that you have not and that you have never heard of organisational politics. Below, RCI Success offers some guidelines you can follow. Any negative consequences of utilising these guidelines are not the fault of RCI Success. The onus lies solely on you.

1. Get Everything in Writing

When you are communicating with different levels of management, and an important message is received, you should record it in writing. All correspondence regarding this instruction should be in writing. This allows you to keep your superiors informed of the actions you are taking in response to their instructions and also to demonstrate that you are doing as directed and not pursuing your own personal agenda.

For example, your manager, Aden, instructed you to raise all costs of motor vehicle accessories by 0.5 per cent and to inform all key dealers and stockholders. You follow these instructions, and as a result, there is a backlash against your company. Aden asks why you told them of the coming cost rise. Confused at his anger, you reply, "I was only following what you told me to do." Upper management hears of the backlash and the negative effect it has on key relationships with dealers, and you are blamed.

Although it is unfair to blame you, in the political realm of the organisation, you are to blame. So how do you avoid a similar situation? You get everything in writing!

This is what you should have done: after taking verbal instructions from Aden, you should have written him an email:

> *Good afternoon, Aden,*
>
> *As discussed at this afternoon's meeting, I will begin to inform Y, Z, and A of our 0.5 per cent cost increase of all motor vehicle accessories. I will also notify other necessary key stakeholders, following our core stakeholder list. Please let me know if you require me to take any additional action in order to make this transition as smooth as possible. I will keep you updated with their responses (if any).*

Sending this email before you begin notifying stakeholders gives Aden the opportunity to correct you, if needed. It also reinforces that notifying the key stakeholders is the appropriate action to take and was definitely discussed at the meeting. This is one way to protecting yourself.

2. Read and Reread

There is nothing worse than sending an email to the wrong person or selecting "cc" rather than "bcc." Double-check everything in your email and the recipients to ensure you are sending the correct information to the designated recipient. Once you are satisfied, hit the Send button. Mark emails which require urgent attention with a "!" in Outlook or in a similar way in other email programs.

Address people and attachments directly in the email. This way, if you forget to send the attachment or it is not received or acknowledged by the recipient, they cannot blame you. You highlighted its existence in the body of your email. It also lets them know that an attachment was intended to be sent, so if they did not receive it, it is their responsibility to make sure they received it.

The game is plagued with shifting responsibility from yourself onto someone else. This can range from minute issues to taking major action which could threaten a company's future. Following the above two steps can make the difference between being blamed or being blameless.

I Want to Be My Own Boss

After reading all the previous information, you may be feeling slightly overwhelmed. You may think that surely finding a job and keeping it is not that hard. Or the stress of dealing with your boss might be driving you to the edge of insanity and has convinced you that you could be a better boss than him or her.

A lot of people experience these thoughts throughout their working life. And this leads them to think, *Why not become my own boss?* If you're one of those considering opening up your own business or becoming a sole trader, that's great! There is nothing more thrilling than being in charge of your own finances. You no longer have to follow orders, and so you start investing money and time in developing your own pot of gold. Simple, right? Wrong! Taking on your own venture is challenging and exhausting for a number of reasons.

Firstly, when you are starting out or if you are a sole employee, you have the responsibility of all the work. No one is there to share the workload. You might fancy this idea, but it can be a struggle to stay motivated when you're by yourself. Keep this in mind if you cannot work without others in your company. If you prefer to work solo and do not foresee this as a problem, you can move on to the second reason.

Secondly, developing your own ideas is exciting. However, since they are your own ideas, it is difficult to be critical and to determine which ideas are realistic and appropriate. Using a business colleague or utilising free government support from Business Enterprise Centres (BEC) can assist you with this process. (More on BEC is below.)

Owning a business means you will be held accountable for legal obligations such as tax, GST, and superannuation contributions (if applicable).

Research your obligations before starting out, as this aspect of business can be very stressful. Further preparation includes but is not limited to the following:

- Acquiring an ABN and an ASIC number
- Securing a unique domain name
- Opening a separate business banking account
- Applying for a government grant
- Applying for business loans (if needed)
- Applying for any necessary licences or permits

To help organise and begin developing your business, there are some standard processes and documents most entrepreneurs complete. Basic documents include but are not limited to the following:

- A business plan
- A marketing plan
- A Strengths, Weaknesses, Opportunities, Threats (SWOT) analysis
- Website content and design development
- A business card design and printing
- Office acquirement (if necessary)
- HR policies and procedures (if necessary)
- A succession plan
- An emergency management and recovery plan

Business Enterprise Centres is a government not-for-profit organisation which provides start-up and small businesses with advisory services, workshops, and training opportunities. It is a great resource, as it can assist you with the above documents and ensure you're on the right track.

Once all the above documents have been completed, you need to start putting your plans into action. One of the first steps I took for RCI Success was increasing its digital footprint.

Creating a Digital Footprint

There are many free avenues you can take to develop your digital footprint and thereby increase your business's exposure. Create various social media profiles—such as LinkedIn, Facebook, Twitter, and a blog—and utilise these platforms to promote your business.

Enlisting your business in as many free business directories as possible increases traffic to your website and allows your target market to find you. For example, posting an ad on Gumtree has proven to be quite effective for RCI Success.

Writing a blog with keywords and tags increases your chances of being found in a web engine search if your website is not undergoing search engine optimisation (SEO) practises. Add images of video footage that appeal to your audience. These are some no-cost ways for potential clients to find you.

You also need to consider that potential clients in Generation Y use their mobile phones to find and engage business services and purchase products online. Any digital footprint you create must be mobile-phone compatible.

Social Media for Business

Social media can act as a great kick-start to your online marketing. It is useful not only for active job searchers, but also for businesses trying to source new clients and maintain client relationships. Use social media as an interactive platform to ask clients questions about what they think and believe about the industry you are in, general news events, and topics which interest them (which requires researching target markets). Posts, blogs, and social media pages should not be just about promoting your business, but also about offering free resources and product or service updates. The majority of your social media effort must be designated towards developing relationships and interactions with clients and potential clients. By becoming personal and being seen as a trusted business, you can see your sales increase.

Securing a Domain Name

Purchasing a domain name so you can use your business name in your URL is essential for securing your digital space. It will also help potential customers find you without confusion. Although website development is not one of the top priorities on a start-up business's agendas, taking this step will prevent coming across issues in the future.

Website Design and Development

Before you consider purchasing design and development packages or services, consider what content-management systems (CMS) are most user-friendly. You must conduct research on which CMS generate the top rankings on Google, as Google is the number-one search engine connecting potential clients to businesses. Make sure whatever option you decide to use, the back end of your website allows you to manipulate metadata, page title tags, URL structures, and uploading of images and videos.

Constantly updating your site with new content and images is a must to maintain or increase your Google rankings. Do not steal competitors' content, as Google will not like this and your ratings will fall quickly. Utilising as many free tools as possible, including Google analytics (www. google.com/analytics), which can help you track how your clients found you as well as your website's performance.

Business Cards

This is a great and necessary networking tool for you to give to clients and potential clients. You should always carry some of your cards with you. You never know who will be in need of your services or products. If it is not yet within your budget to design and order professional business cards, order some free ones. These have standard designs; they do not give you the option of uploading your own images or logos. However, these are useful for sharing your contact details. Vistaprint offer 250 free standard business cards. Postage and handling costs are not included.

Developing a Recordkeeping System

Accurate recordkeeping of sales, purchases, and unanticipated expenses will help you identify areas of profits and losses that are occurring and what type of improvements to your business must be implemented. Your recordkeeping system does not need to be complex. You can use Excel databases for recording invoices and purchase order numbers, costs, if payment has been received or if you have made a payment, the date payments are due, and how much money was made or lost. You can also have multiple spreadsheets.

When you meet clients, you can issue receipts or tax invoices using a tax invoice book from the local newsagency. This provides you with a hard copy. For electronic transfers, invoices can be made using accounting software such as MYOB or Xero. If using this software is not an option, make an invoice template in Word. A legitimate tax invoice must have the following features:

- "Tax Invoice" on the top with an invoice reference number
- The ABN with contact details: email, phone and/or fax number, name of company, physical or postal address
- Date
- Payment details
- A clear description of the products or services provided
- Amount of GST (if applicable)

You can also include these:

- Business logo
- Date the invoice is due

After you have created this in Word, save the document as a PDF in a designated "unpaid invoices" folder. By saving the document as a PDF, you are limiting the receivers' ability to change it. It is also difficult for them to copy and paste your logo. Once you have emailed or mailed the invoice, record the date of issue in your database with a reminder to follow up on it and all other outstanding invoices.

Having an accurate recordkeeping system is essential for start-up businesses. Records allow you to forecast cash flow for the following months and highlight immediate payment or cash flow issues. Do not underestimate how important recordkeeping is for business growth.

Maintaining accurate records is a legal requirement for tax purposes. It is also a buffer if you were to be audited; if you cannot justify your tax return submissions, as you do not have the necessary records, you or your business can be heavily fined with large interest rates attached. If you are unsure of your recordkeeping requirements, visit www.ato.gov.au. An understanding of these obligations will prevent accidental tax evasion and will help you decide whether running a business is too stressful or worth the challenge.

Accounting Software

If your business is slowly growing, you have employees, and you use common suppliers and clients, then investing in a basic accounting software is a smart move. It allows you to create supplier, customer, and employee cards so you can track purchases, sales, and payroll practises. It also allows you to calculate how much super contributions and taxes must be paid in each quarter's BAS statement (once you have annual turnover of over $75,000).

Accounting software allows you to generate reports on all functions, which assists your cash-flow management. Software can also be linked directly to bank accounts so incoming and outgoing invoices or payslips can be made. Customised company invoices can also be designed to give your company a professional persona.

Cloud-based software provides an option for backing up your information. This gives you peace of mind regarding document theft or property damage. Popular small-business software include MYOB and Xero. Training workshops are available in many locations and are recommended for beginners to ensure accurate recordkeeping.

Client Database

Business development calls or follow-up calls are essential for keeping previous clients and generating new business leads. Excel spreadsheets are great for logging contact details, the dates you last made contact, and the nature of the conversation or email. You can also use it to track how many clients are coming to you from your website, from your social media profiles, or by word of mouth. You can gather this information by asking clients, "How did you hear about our services or our products?" when you first speak to them. This information is crucial in determining where you should allocate more money and resources in terms of marketing or business development.

Filing System

All documents should be neatly filed and retrievable by all employees. The system should be noted. Filing cabinets with manila folders can separate aspects of business functioning. Your system should be specific to your business, and the files should be constantly updated or refiled.

Private information must be protected electronically by using passwords or security software. All hard copy files must be under lock and key. What is deemed "private information' is outlined in the Privacy Act 1998.

Mission and Value Statements

Clients and potential employees want to know an organisation has a sense of direction and a set of values which guide its business activities and conduct. Understanding what direction you would like as a professional and your new organisation to follow in the future is key to a business's success. How an organisation will develop and grow should be planned well before a business launch. This is known as a mission statement and is often available to the public via a website or slogan.

Values incorporate a set of ethics or a code of conduct which the organisation and its representatives are committed to upholding. Values can also include a sense of responsibility to the surrounding community, supporting environmental sustainability, or increasing awareness of a social issue via volunteer participation or the organisation's sponsorship. Making an organisation's values public is part of larger marketing campaigns. An organisation's values also are a part of a potential candidate's evaluation of your organisation—whether they consider you to be a suitable employer or not. Like a mission statement, values must be considered in the development stage of a business's conceptualisation.

Business Development Methods

Once you have assessed your finances and allocated a budget towards business development activities, you must decide what activities would be the most effective within your budget. These activities extend beyond the free avenues discussed above. Methods range from online advertising campaigns to running free workshops.

Google AdWords is a cost-effective method of increasing exposure and traffic to your website. Facebook advertisements are used to generate likes to business pages. However, the quality of the likes is not guaranteed; people who like the page may or may not be genuinely interested in your business's services or products.

Banner advertising entails linking an advertisement on a webpage to your website. Some websites offer affiliate programs in which you add a website's links and its banners to your own webpage. In this way, you drive traffic to your partner's business. You earn a commission on how many clicks and business leads are generated from your webpage's banners and links. Installation is easy; it merely requires embedding banner codes into your pages and choosing the appropriate banner size.

Provide free resources on your website or at conferences. An example is RCI Success conducting a free cover-letter writing workshop on a university campus. Before and after the workshop, we provide information about RCI Success, contact details if further assistance is requested, and an opportunity to buy this book. Although this costs RCI Success money and time, the payoff can be great, with multiple client leads generated or books purchased.

Partnership arrangements allow your business to be promoted in exchange for services or products provided for free or at a minimal rate. These relationships are bidirectional and can greatly increase your client base.

Advertising

Familiarise yourself with the Australian Competition and Consumer Commission (ACCC) standards of advertising. As a business, you do not want to be unfair and have competitive products or services as a result of dishonest representations. Compliance is monitored and enforced by the Australian Advertising Standards Bureau. A code of ethics is available on its website: http://www.adstandards.com.au/.

Community Involvement

In exchange for your business's donations or volunteer participation, non-profit organisations or associations will promote your business using collateral materials, such as listing you on their website as a sponsor or supporter, referring you to their clients, or using your logo on their own materials (if you're a partner).

Developing Human Resource Policies and Procedures

Human resource policies, procedures, and documents are an important component of any business. They protect employees and the business from legal liability and serve as a means of increasing overall employee satisfaction and performance. Protection extends from employee health and safety to business information security to mandatory human resource documents which include but are not limited to the following:

- Flexible working arrangements
- Human resource manual
- Code of conduct
- Worker health and safety policy
- Drug and alcohol policy
- Nondisclosure agreement

- Computer policy
- Disciplinary action scheme
- Social media policy
- Recruitment and selection manual

Employee satisfaction is nurtured when a business has policies and procedures which recognise their working achievements and help them achieve their career goals. Performance appraisal systems, training and development, and internal promotion opportunities encourage employees to strive for excellence. They provide security by recognising and rewarding good work, and they teach industry and work-related skills.

Regular performance appraisals allow upper management to determine whether employees are performing well and poorly. Upper management then has the ability to reward efforts and issue disciplinary actions if required.

Template Agreements

These agreements outline the terms of service or terms of use of your business. Standard documents include privacy statements, refund policies, contracts for services rendered, and limited warrantees. So why have them?

- *Agreements protect your business from legality issues.* They establish the rules of business before customers and other businesses engage your services or purchase your products. This reduces disputes and outlines where your business's responsibility ends.
- *Agreements limit your liability.* By having a "terms of engagement" which customers and businesses must sign or agree to before business undertakings, it limits their ability to sue if they are not satisfied with the services or products provided.
- *Agreements protect your business property.* Agreements make your customers and other businesses aware that they do not have permission to redistribute, use or copy your intellectual property, products, or services without your explicit permission.

Like human resource documents, template agreements must use unambiguous language which is easily understood. If you believe terms could be misunderstood, clarify the terms with a "Definitions" section in the agreement. Customers must also be aware that agreements exist and where they can be found. These agreements must be available before and after a sale or a service.

You must include what your business will provide in return for payment and attach a limitation of liability. If you're going to draft this agreement yourself, do not copy it from other businesses. Your template must be tailored to your business, and the terms must be clear to every customer and other businesses.

Competition and Consumer Law

It is essential that you understand the Australia's Competition and Consumer Act 2010 (CCA), which names the rights and obligations of businesses when they are dealing with their customers and other businesses. An understanding ensures you respect the welfare of Australians and prevent your business from misleading, deceptive, or unconscionable conduct. The act also includes guidelines on appropriate action for refunds and product safety.

Competition and consumer laws must be utilised by businesses. These laws set the benchmark in business conduct, such as refund regulations, information on deceptive advertising, and pricing guidelines for products and services. If you're considering opening a business, become familiar with your obligations. For further information, visit www.accc.gov.au.

Becoming a Justice of the Peace

A justice of the peace (JP) acts as a government representative servicing the community voluntarily. You can also become a JP if it is necessary for your business to continue functioning. Becoming a JP as a business owner can be advantageous in certain industries when multiple statutory declarations, certification of original documents, or witnessing affidavits are necessary.

Application Process to Become a JP

Before filling out the application form, you must first determine whether you are eligible. Eligibility requirements differ from state to state.

Once you have determined that you are eligible within your state, fill out the application form. This includes providing two written and signed references from professionals within specified industries who have known you for over two years. Your references cannot be related to you. Once signed by a local member of Parliament, your application will take between six and eight weeks to process.

The JP application differs across Australian states. The above information is applicable in NSW. For further information, visit http://www.jp.nsw.gov.au/.

Being an Entrepreneur

Being an entrepreneur is difficult. You're responsible for everything, at least at the beginning. It is a huge learning experience; you begin to understand what works to gain clients and what does not work for you and your business. Building a strong client base is one of the most difficult tasks a start-up faces.

Firstly, your new organisation, does not have a history of offering services or products. As an entrepreneur, it is your job to convince clients or customers that they can place their trust in you. When they do, you must deliver. It is hard to stop a dissatisfied client from spreading the word about you as a professional or your business services or products.

Secondly, you are discovering the most efficient ways to deliver a service or product to your clients in a way that is economically viable for the business and satisfies your clients' needs. Start-up organisations rarely have high efficiency straight away and often make mistakes with their first few clients. This limits a start-up's ability to build a strong client base in the beginning phase of business.

On top of all your other responsibilities, you are the person who must sell your products or services. Developing a sales pitch with which you are able to concisely explain the value of your business and what differentiates you from your competition is a must. Differentiating your business from others should have been discussed or determined before launching the business; it should be a part your business plan and SWOT analysis.

Networking must be a part of your everyday activities. If networking is outside your comfort zone, begin practicing with friends and previous colleagues, telling about your business and asking if they could recommend your services. Once you have a little practise, begin attending industry-related or business-related social or networking events. Carry with you plenty of business cards and a place to keep business cards given to you. You will begin to see the value of networking, as word-of-mouth referrals are valued more highly by potential clients than advertising or forms of marketing.

Ways to Keep Your Employees Happy

Employers must be aware that their employee turnover rate and any associated costs can be managed by keeping their employees happy and feeling appreciated. Employees must understand what they can expect from their employer, such as a work environment that nurtures high productivity and also encourages a healthy work-life balance.

Before reading the employer methods below, you must first ask what makes you happy in an organisation? What is it about your job or your working environment which makes you unhappy? It is critical for employers to adopt an employee perspective before adopting the suggestions below.

Have an Organisational Mission

This gives perspective to employees' day-to-day work. It helps them visualise how their individual achievements are important contributions which drive the company towards attaining its mission. Without a mission, employees struggle to grasp the purpose of their work. If employees cannot see the reason for or the impact of their contributions, motivation and enthusiasm levels drop. When this happens, your employees are no longer happy. Organisations should make their employees, the surrounding community, and their major clients aware of their mission statement.

Employee Trust

Employers must be careful not to trusting their employees with too much, such as by providing passwords and user names for the back end of websites, accounting software, or banking accounts. But they also must avoid too little trust by micromanaging employees' day-to-day tasks. The amount of autonomy and trust an employee receives is a major determinant of whether an employee is happy or unhappy in his or her organisation.

Partnering with Other Businesses

Supporting or having established bidirectional business relationships permits you to offer additional benefits to employees in order to keep them happy. For example, your construction company might partner with a health and fitness organisation. In return for providing discounted building services, they can offer your employees free memberships or access to gym facilities. This optimises their ability to maintain a healthy work and lifestyle balance. (It has been shown that healthier employees are more productive and enthusiastic towards work than their colleagues who do not engage in regular exercise and healthy eating.) These benefits are a common way of making employees happier in your organisation.

Flexible Working Arrangements

Australians appreciate their downtime and the freedom to pursue recreational activities outside of work. Employees also have multiple commitments, such as volunteer involvement and family, and thereby require flexible working hours. With a high demand on casual and part-time employment, an employer which embraces this trend will retain more employees. By offering flexible working arrangements as an option, your employers will continue to keep their employees happy.

Continual Feedback Loop

It is difficult to feel confident in the quality of your work when you receive feedback only once a year at a scheduled performance appraisal. Continuous communication between an employer and its employees can dispel doubts when employee targets are being met and the work meets the expectations of upper management.

Conducting a Termination Interview

As the employer, it is your responsibility to decide when an employee is no longer suitable in her current position. The reasons for your decision could be that she is disrupting the workflow, is not an organisational fit, has difficulty working with other team members, or is not satisfying her job requirements. Regardless of your reasons, immediate action is necessary, but this action must be well planned and handled delicately. Terminations are often met by lawsuits against unfair dismissals. Abiding by Australian legislation, and in particular the Discrimination Act (Cth) of 1975, must be a standard in any organisation and carried out by its representatives or human-resource manager.

Human-resource managers must ensure that termination is in the best interests of the organisation and not someone's own personal interests. Terminations cost any organisation a considerable amount of money for recruiting and training other suitable candidates. With the time and resources devoted to finding a replacement, terminations are a hassle not only for the HR manager, but also for the organisation.

With all these considerations, a termination is an important aspect of the exiting process. It can prevent both hurt feelings and the terminating employee destroying the organisation's reputation and/or property. This is a sensitive issue, and HR managers or organisational representatives quite often do not know how to handle the process and avoid humiliating or angering the employee.

Organise a one-on-one meeting between the HR manager and the employee. Ensure that the meeting is conducted in a quiet setting where others cannot overhear. Keep the nature of the meeting neutral, and do not tell colleagues of your intentions to terminate the employee; you do not want gossip to spread in the office.

Termination interviews must get straight to the point. Sit the employee down and explain the reasons you have arranged the meeting. Do not point the blame or attribute his performance (if poor) to his personality. Focus on the aspects of his behaviour which are not up to par. Then allow him a chance to respond. Do not interrupt the employee, and allow him time to explain himself. He may offer an insight into specific circumstances which you were not aware of, which could prevent or postpone his termination.

The employee will be in an emotional state. As the HR manager, respect his reaction. After giving him a few moments to compose himself, begin outlining the steps he will need to follow after the meeting. This could range from gathering his personal belongings and relinquishing his access to accounts and company information. It may also include liaising with payroll so he can organise and receive any entitled payouts.

The Challenges of Terminations

A termination is especially difficult within a small team when the boss or HR manager has been worked closely with the employee being terminated. Small businesses often face this problem, especially when they need to reduce labour costs, and the only option is to downsize and thereby make employees redundant.

Employees can become angry and want to take revenge against their former employer personally and/or against the organisation. This is why it is imperative to change user names and passwords former employees had access to. If they have continued access, they could easily cause chaos ranging from shutting down a website to tarnishing the organisation's reputation by sending inappropriate emails using the organisation's email address.

Litigation can follow against the organisation and associated HR personnel under the notion of "unfair dismissal." If this occurs, it is up to the employer to provided relevant evidence and documentation that the dismissal was fair. Litigation is a major reason HR managers must conduct careful termination interview. If an employee is made completely aware and understands the valid reasons behind her dismissal, she will be less motivated to make a claim.

There are a multitude of challenges HR managers and organisations can face with terminated employees. When conducting termination interviews and the processes afterwards, they must allow the employee to leave the organisation without feeling humiliated, embarrassed, or thinking the dismissal was not justified.

Chapter 9

A Psychological Perspective

Now for the really interesting part of this book. The previous chapters focused on the practical aspects of being successful in landing a job. This chapter focuses solely on the processes which occur in a candidate and an interviewer. They shed light on automatic psychological and physiological responses to body language and how these are processed by the human brain. You can use this understanding to your advantage and land a job quickly.

The Power of Words

People say that actions speak louder than words, and it's true. However, the power of words should not be underestimated. Multiple studies using fMRI scans of the human brain demonstrate that words are just as powerful in how people feel and process a new stimuli and how they respond. This is due to the language centre of the brain being linked to the amygdala and the hippocampus, which are specialised for processing emotions. With these interneural connections, there is a bidirectional interaction between language and emotions; language influences emotions, and emotions influence language.

A single negative word can trigger dozens of stress-producing hormones, including cortisol and epinephrine. These hormones can disrupt brain functioning. Negative words signal to the brain that danger is imminent, initiating a physiological response of either fight or flight.

Although this occurs on a miniscule scale, people subconsciously process these physiological reactions as how much they like a person. If you're in an interview, you want their brains to like you as much as possible. Substituting negative words for positive words will help their brains along.

Background Information

Whenever words are heard, a normal human brain processes them in a standard way. The words are heard and are sent to the temporal lobe in the cerebral cortex to be processed. The temporal lobe is a section of the brain specialised for processing language. The left temporal lobe is specialised for understanding spoken language. They are interconnected with the limbic system, which include the amygdala, hippocampus, and olfactory cortex (provides our perception of smell). The limbic system has primitive origins and is the primary emotion centre in the brain. It regulates fear, empathy, and feelings of emotional closeness. With these centres being strongly tied to memory, first impressions are not easily forgotten and elicit strong emotional responses from us.

Using the Power of Words

The power of words on emotions has been recognised and manipulated by people of power, the media, artists, and the everyday salesperson to achieve agendas and influence decisions. By recognising the impact words have on people's emotional state, you can influence their decision-making processes, as the majority of decisions are made using "gut feelings" rather than logic.

There are three different routes used in decision making:

- *Habitual decision making,* such as low-involvement purchasing decisions, low-risk products. Examples of these include walking into a department store and buying the same toothpaste you always buy. There is little thinking or emotion involved in this decision.
- *Shallow decision making,* such as limited-involvement purchasing decision which are highly influenced by emotions; thought processes are limited. Marketing campaigns which target this type

of decision making include catchy tunes and jingles. The words used are simple and straight to the point.

- *Extended decision making,* such as high-involvement purchasing decisions involving high-price, unfamiliar products. This type of decision making revolves around high cognitive activity, with people weighing the options and using logic. Emotions do not affect in-depth processing as much as shallow processing.

The most notable example of word users in a business context is telemarketers. Telemarketers recognise the power of words and so manipulate their language to appeal to their target market. After years of refinement and my own personal research, I have developed a list of ten or so power words and phrases which should be avoided. Read through the list and see if you agree. How do you feel about these words? Now compare these words to the phrases listed? Can you feel the power difference?

Positive Words

1. You
2. Money
3. Guaranteed
4. Save
5. New
6. Love
7. Proven
8. Discovery
9. Safety
10. Easy

Phrases to Avoid

1. How are you?
2. I'll be honest with you.
3. No obligations.
4. Make my day.
5. You're not going to find a better deal anywhere else.

This knowledge is applicable when using any type of medium, whether it is email, over the phone, or face-to-face. Using positive language will help you communicate your message so that it is well be received by listeners. Below is an exercise for you to complete. Say each word slowly out loud, and try to decide which words are positive or negative.

Exercise 1. Positive Words

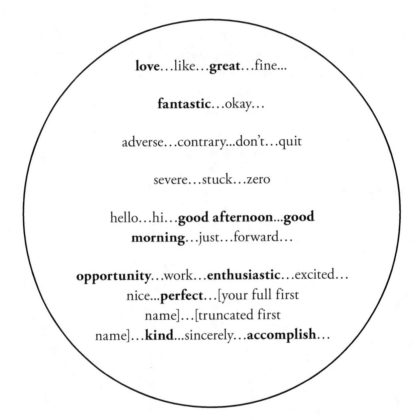

love...like...**great**...fine...

fantastic...okay...

adverse...contrary...don't...quit

severe...stuck...zero

hello...hi...**good afternoon**...**good morning**...just...forward...

opportunity...work...**enthusiastic**...excited... nice...**perfect**...[your full first name]...[truncated first name]...**kind**...sincerely...**accomplish**...

After completing this exercise, it is wise to consider your own learning. When you learn a word or have an experience with an object or person, you form associations. These associations remain entrenched within the context in which you learnt the word. When you hear the same word, your prior learning comes into effect. Many psychologists use this for "priming" a participant—*eliciting his or her learning to induce a certain emotional or physiological reaction.* Priming words automatically activate the stored representations of all words related due to massive previous learning. This directly inhibits or increases the chances of words being either positive or negative. Keep these factors in mind when you read the two examples below.

Positive Telephone Conversation

Here is an example of a telemarketer attempting to make a sales pitch.

Negative

> *Hi, Melvin. How are you today? My name is Arash from Security Essentials, I'm just calling in regards to your existing home security plan. Do you have a few moments to discuss it?*

Positive

> *Good afternoon, Melvin. This is Arash Marque calling from Security Essentials. The reason for my call is we are offering free installation improvements on your existing security plan. Do you have a few moments to discuss these options?*

Notice that the second blurb is more powerful. They had the same message but used different words. Substituting negative words for positive words decreases anxiety and the number of negative subconscious thoughts you and the recipients of the message experience.

Words and the Brain

There are two main systems within the brain which regulate our physiological responses to foreign or confronting stimuli. Understanding how these two systems operate independently and together can help you understand what is happening within your own body as a job candidate as well as your interviewer(s) body. These two systems are ARAS and BIS.

ARAS is the abbreviation for the Ascending Reticular Activation System in the brain. This is a network of fibres extending from the spinal cord to the thalamus of the brain at a level below the cortex. The ARAS is involved in attention, concentration, corticol efficiency in learning, conditioning, wakefulness, and attention, while the thalamus is involved in emotional regulation. When you are in an environment with new stimuli, your ARAS becomes highly activated. Your attention to your surroundings becomes heightened whilst elevated corticol levels circulate in your blood. Corticol is a hormone released in association with the typical symptoms of nervousness. You know these as sweating, shaking, butterflies in your stomach, or a dry mouth. Individuals differ in how their corticol levels impede their normal bodily functioning.

BIS stands for Behavioural Inhibition System. This system includes the septum, hippocampus, amygdala, and parts of the frontal cortex used to arouse states of fear. The amygdala and hippocampus in themselves are specialist areas responsible for fear and empathy regulation.

The ARAS and BIS systems work together to manage stress levels and physiological reactions when a person is confronted with a new stimulus. The BIS works with higher centres (complex thinking) in "checking mode" to determine what meaning a stimulus might have. If the organism's checking registers a threat, the BIS takes control, leading to withdrawal; you feel obliged to run, leave the situation, or avoid contact with the confronting stimuli.

When an interviewer meets a candidate for the first time, these two systems are on the alert. As you, the candidate, register the new stimulus, your brain assesses whether the interviewer is a threat or not, and whether you're a positive or negative addition to his or her environment. The BIS interprets the stimulus as either threatening or safe. So now when you meet an interviewer, you will know that whether or not she takes a liking to you is due to automatic complex processes. She is completely unaware of why she develops gut feelings about certain candidates. Now that you have an understanding, you can use this to your advantage.

Candidates which are well presented and smile with their teeth are perceived as less threatening. This has evolutionary roots: foreign tribal members showed their teeth as a sign of peace as they approached other clans. Being clean and having no hair hiding your face means that you approach honestly and are making no attempt to hide your identity or deceive others about your intentions.

You now know why you experience symptoms of nervousness when under stress. You have elevated levels of corticol in your blood as you enter a foreign environment and situation. You can naturally decrease these levels by using relaxation exercises before the interview. You can also make the interview situation less foreign to you by practicing mock interviews with a friend—practicing the entire time as if it were a real interview.

Taking these steps is an effective method of deceasing your own BIS and ARAS activation levels. Once you relax, your interviewers should also relax and recognise you as a positive addition to their environment.

Your Personality and Your Job

There has been a constant debate about personality since psychology was deemed an area worth investigating. Some scholars argue that we are born with a "blank slate," and our experiences fill up this empty vessel to create who we are. Others posit that we are born with a basic temperament, and so our personality remains stable as we grow. Another perspective incorporates the two: we are born with a biological disposition and our temperament, which provides us with our initial characteristics, and we are moulded by our nurture and physical environments.

It is unknown which theory is correct. Regardless, psychologists have developed frameworks in an attempt to categorise personality characteristics into traits. One of the most accepted personality frameworks is the Five Factor Model of Personality.

Five-Factor Model of Personality

The Five Factor Model of Personality uses the acronym of OCEAN:

Openness to experiences: People with this characteristic have soaring imaginations and deep insights into different situations. They are also naturally inquisitive and have a broad range of interests.

Conscientiousness: These people are able to control impulses and to be thoughtful about how their actions affect themselves and others. They display goal-directed behaviours and quite often have perfectionistic tendencies.

Extraversion: This trait includes gregariousness, a need to be sociable, talkative, and assertive. Extraverts are highly expressive and seek out physical and emotional intimacy with others in a variety of environments.

Agreeableness: People high in agreeableness are seen as peacekeepers. They believe in being harmonious with others through kindness, trust, and affection.

Neuroticism: Attributes associated with neuroticism include emotional instability, anxiety, moodiness, and proneness to stress and bouts of depression in the face of unexpected situations.

Each of the five personality traits represents an extreme on a continuum. For example, if you lie at the high end of extraversion as you are a social butterfly, while lying at the low extreme makes you a major introvert. Studies have found that these personality traits are universal cross-culturally and so can be used by anyone reading this book.

Use this model to try to understand yourself. Where do you fall on each OCEAN spectrum? Are you at the high level of the extraversion spectrum? Certain organisations engage psychologist services to perform personality assessments on shortlisted candidates to determine their suitability to the role based the ideal levels of each OCEAN trait. If you understand each trait and the typical characteristics associated with each one, you will be know what type of answer the interviewer is trying to elicit from you or the trait the question is assessing.

By looking at job descriptions and the listed characteristics employers desire, you can determine whether you're suitable for a role or not. You can also determine whether you are suited to highly stressful roles or slow-paced roles based on the amount of stimulation you're comfortable with.

Final Thoughts

If you use OCEAN, you do not have to think you're an extravert and that's that. The degree to which you express your personality traits depends upon the situation you're in. For example, if you're in a library with your friends, although you might usually be talkative (high on extraversion), in this situation you are very quiet. From an outsider looking in, without any clue into the social norm that you remain quiet in a library out of respect for others, they might perceive you as an introvert, as you are not engaging others around you. Situational confines are important determinants to what degree a trait is expressed.

Now, taking this analogy from an enlightened perspective, you should not attribute people's behaviour to their personality, as multiple situational and contextual factors influence their behaviour. If you do this, and we all do or have done so in the past, you are committing an attributional error.

We constantly make attributional errors without even realising it. When you're in a shopping centre going around and around, looking for a car spot, and then you see someone who has double-parked, you may think that person is selfish to the core. You're filled with rage, as one of those spots could have been yours, and now because of that person you have to keep driving in search of another.

By saying that person must be selfish, you have committed an attributional error. You've associated her behaviour of double-parking with her personality. But you do not know she had double-parked. This person could be genuinely selfish or a very kind person who double-parked because she was in a hurry.

This example should challenge your idea of personality; it is not as black and white as most people believe. Personalities and people cannot be put into boxes. We constantly exhibit behaviour specific to our situations and so move fluidly along the trait continuums. By understanding this, you will be wiser and more accepting towards people in general, as first impressions can be extremely inaccurate.

The Power of Body Language

You can subtly use body language to further your career, increase sales, and even be more successful in an interview. Yep, that's right! With nonverbal communication contributing to up to 75 per cent of what you're actually saying, understanding your body language and how it's perceived by others will help you master it. Mastering it moulds your body language to project a message which is desirable and favourable in an interview.

Gestures to Avoid in Interviews

The physical gestures we use are processed subconsciously by others. Projecting the right image and messages requires being aware of your body language and being able to differentiate between the positive and the negative. With a little understanding and some practise, you can overcome the gestures which can let you down in an interview.

- *Crossing your arms:* This is a defensive pose. Some people also interpret it as a signal of egotism. Substitute crossed your arms for open body language; show your palms and rest your hands in your lap.
- *Scratching your head or neck:* This is subconsciously interpreted as a signal that you're being deceitful or are experiencing doubt or uncertainty about something you just said or are listening to. Avoid scratching your head or neck when you are interviewed, especially when responding to a question. Try to keep your hands firmly in your lap or on the table when communicating with the interviewer.
- *Wiping sweaty hands on your clothing:* We've all been there: we're nervous and our hands become inconveniently sweaty. Resist the instinct to wipe them on your clothing in plain sight of the interviewer. This will highlight your nervousness. Try to relax. They will not know you're sweaty until you go to shake their hand when the interview has finished, giving you plenty of time to relax.
- *Shifting your body weight between feet:* Before and after an interview, you will stand up, shake hands with the interviewers,

and thank them for their time. Sometimes they will continue the conversation as you both are standing. Resist the urge to shift your body weight from foot to foot. This suggests that you're feeling uneasy. People also see this as an intention to end the conversation as swiftly as possible.

- *Slouching shoulders:* When seated, keep your shoulders back. In an interview, this indicates that you're attentive, self-confident, and ready to answer any question they throw your way. Slouching could be seen as introversion, a lack of self-confidence, or low self-esteem. As you ensure your shoulders are not slouched, you will also feel more confident and project that to the interviewer.

- *Posture:* Your posture also relates to your slouching shoulders. Whether you're standing, walking, or sitting in a chair, your posture is interpreted by others. It's a sign of your confidence and how you're feeling about yourself at that moment. Keep your feet firmly planted on the floor. Keep your shoulders pulled back and your head up, and greet people with eye contact and a smile.

- *Sitting on the edge of your chair:* When you're in an interview, you want the interviewers to think that you're at ease in your own skin. If you seem as though you're not, they could associate this with you not being capable of fulfilling the job responsibilities, especially if you are being interviewed for a leadership position. Sitting on the edge of your chair is an apprehensive stance. When you lean into the conversation, remain firmly pressed to the back of your chair, but lean forward with your back and shoulders. If your chair starts to tilt, this is a hint that you need to lean firmly back into it.

- *Stroking your chin:* People often stroke their chin when they are contemplating or thinking about a difficult question. If you're asked a difficult question in an interview and you touch your chin, the interviewer may subconsciously interpret this as you judging him or her rather than contemplating the question asked.

- *Touching your face during the interview:* Subconsciously, face touching while speaking is interpreted as deception, especially when you touch your nose or cover your mouth when you speak. Covering your mouth while speaking is seen as subconsciously stopping yourself from telling a lie. When in an interview, keep your hands in your lap or clasped on the table. This will prevent you from fidgeting and touching your face.

- *Leaning away from people:* When you're interested in a person or a conversation, you start to lean in towards the person. This is a sign of interest and is positive body language. In an interview, when asked a question, lean in. If the interviewer leans towards you, also lean in. Not leaning forward can be interpreted as a sign of disinterest.

- *Holding objects between you and the interviewer:* Holding objects directly in front of you serves as a physical barrier to communication and interaction. This is not good in an interview or when meeting a client or stranger for the first time. When possible, hold objects to your side.

- *Faking a smile:* Everyone has the ability to recognise the difference between a fake and a genuine smile. Fake smiles are associated with a deceitful character and untrustworthiness. Do not force yourself to smile. Be genuinely happy to meet your interviewers, as they are providing an opportunity for employment. If you can't muster a genuine smile, perhaps subconsciously you're not as keen on the position as you think.

- *Fidgeting with small objects:* Fidgeting during an interview or playing with your hands is a clear sign of anxiety. This does not project confidence. Monitor your fidgeting by holding your hands in your lap or on the table.

- *Not directly facing your interviewer:* When your body is facing a person or object, this is seen as interest. When you're engaged in conversation, your torso, feet, and face are directly facing the other person. When you are not committed to a conversation or find it uninteresting, your body subconsciously turns, preparing for an exit. Don't give an impression of disinterest through your body's position.

Improving Your Body Language

There is no clear line between positive and negative body language. Body language must be interpreted within its context. The body language you use will differ in terms of who you're interacting with, your environment, and how you're feeling at the moment. With this in mind, there is no specific advice on correct body language—only guides to follow.

- *Slow down:* Take the time to articulate each word you say. If you speak too quickly, you can easily fumble over your words and seem as though you're mumbling. Slow down and speak with confidence. When you're nervous, this is easier said than done. Practise articulating your words.
- *Blink consistently:* Blinking rapidly is a clear sign of anxiety and makes others think that you feel as though you're under pressure or scrutiny. Try not to blink too much!
- *Smile and laugh:* People subconsciously process smiling as being associated with positive personality traits. People who smile more on average are received as warm, trustworthy, and friendly. Sharing a laugh when appropriate with your interviewer will increase your possibility of getting the job.
- *Use hand gestures:* Use your hands to emphasise your point when responding to a question. These should be open gestures with your palms open and facing the interviewer. Avoid quick, big movements, and don't overuse your hands. Use them when making a point and then rest them again on the table or your lap.
- *Proximity:* Note your proximity to interviewers. Usually a table provides an adequate distance, but when you go to greet them or say good-bye, beware of personal boundaries. The intimate space is larger in Western cultures than in Eastern, where people tend to interact while standing or sitting closer to each other. Be aware of cultural norms, and respect people's personal space; space invaders are not well received by anyone.
- *Mirroring:* When two people are engaged in conversation and it is going well, you will notice that their body language is in sync. One of them will lean forward, and the other will instinctively lean

forward. They will drink at the same time or mimic each other's movements. When in an interview, notice whether the interviewers are mimicking your body language. If so, your interview is going well. If not, begin to mimic their body language, and they will subconsciously process this. They will begin to view you more positively. Try it!

With the innate ability to recognise just under 250,000 facial expressions, humans automatically process and interpret visual cues. Making a conscious effort to understand and monitor your own body language can give you an edge in your dealings with people in general and especially interviewers.

Body Language Exercise

This exercise is a piece of cake. All you need to do is go into a busy place like a shopping centre or a popular restaurant and watch how others interact. How are people responding to each other's body language and language (if you can hear it)? Judge their level of intimacy; are they strangers, close friends, or lovers. How are you able to tell? Body language!

Use the points mentioned above to decipher their body language and determine their relationship status. Notice how couples or friends mirror each other's body language. This will reinforce the basic guidelines and increase your understanding. Once you can identify body language signals, begin to pay close attention to yours. Only then can you control and mould it to project the messages that you want.

You will notice that it is easy to spot confident people. Their postures are upright, they maintain steady eye contact, and they use open gestures frequently when they speak. You can then contrast this to those whom are more reserved; their postures are closed, and they speak softly and maintain little eye contact with those they engage with.

Note: You must keep in mind that each person has a repertoire of body language often referred to as his or her baseline. Pay close attention to swift changes in body language rather than the body language itself, as *context* is a huge factor to consider.

An Insight into Why and How We Work

Ever wondered what drives you to wake up in the morning, get dressed, and go to work? Or what part of you keeps searching for employment despite all the rejections? Organisational psychologists have conducted numerous studies into understanding what motivates us in a work environment. I hope to enlighten you and let you see how psychology is just as important in a workplace as it is in other aspects of your life.

Motivation

Motivation is defined as the force that initiates and maintains goal-orientated behaviour. This force can have a biological root: seeking out water to quench your thirst; emotional roots: looking for a partner to serve your need for intimacy; or cognitive roots: studying health sciences so you understand how diabetes affects your body. Psychologists have devised a number of theories to explain what motivation is and why it occurs.

Drive Theory

According to the drive theory, there are three main components of motivation: activation, persistence, and intensity. Activation involves the conscious decision to initiate a behaviour. Persistence is the continued effort to reach a goal despite obstacles and a lack of the resources and extra energy required. Intensity is the vigour and amount of effort dedicated to achieving your goal. These three components collectively form what we know as "motivation."

Intrinsic Motivation vs. Extrinsic Motivation

There are two variants of motivation. *Extrinsic motivation* arises externally from the individual and usually involves rewards, social recognition, status, or monetary gain. You could be extrinsically motivated to get a promotion because of a higher pay package or for the status attached to a title change.

Intrinsic motivation arises within an individual, such as a desire to paint and draw for personal gratification.

Understanding what type of job and industry is of personal interest enables you to be intrinsically motivated to perform well; this is the type of employment you should pursue. It would be best for both you and your potential employer, as your productivity and overall work performance will be higher. However, it has been found that when you constantly engage in your intrinsic activities and begin to gain extrinsic rewards such as money, your interests can lose their intrinsic value. Keep this in mind when you begin to be paid for your passions.

Motivation in Organisations

Employers understand that motivation is linked to rewards in the workplace. Rewards in an organisation refer to the simple principle that people will not work without the right incentives. For an organisation to attract and retain the best human capital, these incentives must be equal or better than their competitors'. This is fundamental for establishing a competitive advantage, so do not think that organisations do not consider your implicit and explicit motivations as an employee. Employers recognise that rewards' most potent role is to continually motivate employees.

Large organisations try to use a holistic approach which includes a combination of intrinsic and extrinsic rewards. These rewards can be divided into three categories: financial, social, and developmental. Organisations develop appropriate rewards for their workforces by assessing the associated advantages and disadvantages in each category.

Type	Advantages:	Disadvantages:
Financial	Performance-related rewards reinforce past performance in the hope it will be reproduced in the future. Gain sharing encourages employees to reach benchmarks if they wish to reap financial rewards. Share purchase plans make employees feel connected and personally responsible if they cause any harm to their organisation. Restricted share plans minimise senior executives exploiting their high position, as their shareholder entitlements will be jeopardised.	Performance-based pay is contingent with risk and instils job insecurity. Tiny gaps in the merit standing of high performance and average performance encourage high turnover rates. Profit sharing can lead to social loafing; employees give less effort towards achieving targets as they believe others will pick up the slack.
Social	Providing rewards based on merit can motivate employees to improve or maintain their current performance level.	Rewards can create an atmosphere of winners and losers, which can dissolve healthy working relationships. People can view the reward as tokenistic and degrading their work.

		Social rewards can imply unintended messages; if high performers are rewarded with additional time off work, then work can be then viewed as negative.
Developmental	Training buffers against high turnover and employees' skill sets "rusting out." Training is a mode of job enrichment and increases intrinsic motivation, job performance, and satisfaction.	Training opportunities are limited. Systematic procedures fairly select those who will undergo training must be enforced.

Pay Secrecy

Organisations understand how remuneration is a major motivation factor for employees. Therefore, what individuals earn should be kept confidential, as remuneration differences amongst employees who have the same job criteria can spawn negative competition and dissolve healthy working relationships. However, the basis for remuneration differences must be transparent to the employees. For instance, the performance thresholds for receiving annual bonuses and the qualifications required to reach a set salary must be made accessible to all employees. When they understand pay packages or hourly rates, it motivates them, as they know how they can increase their pay. Little transparency can deter motivation, increase employee turnover rates, and disturb a sense of organisational justice.

Organisational Learning

Myriads of books, textbooks, journal articles, websites, and blogs are dedicated to the theory of learning. It's quite easy to become lost with terms such as positive and negative reinforcement, contingency, and proximity intervals. For the sake of this book, only learning theory relevant to organisational psychology will be discussed.

Organisational psychologists focus their energies specifically on the precursors to learning. These extend to an employee's readiness and motivation to learn in an organisation. *Readiness* refers to an employee's degree of maturity and previous work experience. "Motivation to learn" is a reference to an employee's recognition that learning is a form of acquiring new information and skills which are necessary to fulfil a job to the best of their ability.

Readiness to Learn

Individuals go through various stages in order to adopt and maintain a new behaviour. These stages are often used to explain the thought patterns involved when people undergo significant changes to their behaviour. Nevertheless, these can be applied to learning in general.

1. *Precontemplation:* When told by a manager or supervisor that you need to undergo additional training or take a course to supplement your workplace learning, you will resist, if you are like most workers. Some believe that they do not need further training and are insulted; they think that management sees them as incompetent to fulfil their job role or that training requires too much time and effort for what it is worth.
2. *Contemplation:* In this stage you begin to acknowledge the benefits of further learning and that there may be a void in your skills and knowledge necessary to carry out the job role— especially if the job role has expanded or changed drastically due to restructuring or downsizing. As part of your contemplation, you begin to weigh the pros and cons of learning. This initiates the preparation stage.

3. *Preparation:* You've accepted that learning is beneficial not only to yourself but also to your organisation. You've begun reading the modules of the training program, have asked others who have completed the training and learned about what they've absorb and its application towards work, or have begun mentally preparing yourself for learning.

4. *Action:* This is the step when you undergo the learning or training. You absorb as much information as you can so that you will be able to apply to your job.

5. *Maintenance:* Now that you've completed the learning, you want to actively apply your newfound knowledge and skills to your job. You actively practise any skills you've gained or improved.

Hopefully, after undergoing these five stages, people recognise the value in learning within an organisation. When they are presented with a new opportunity to learn, they will not be resistant to or ambiguous about a training program's value in the precontemplation stage. In saying this, although everyone undergoes these stages, the degree to which they learn and how effective the training is varies.

Many factors influence a person's readiness to learn. Anything that affects physical or psychological comfort, such as fatigue, stress, anxiety, or fear, can affect a person's readiness to learn. This is why a healthy and nurturing work environment encourages the most efficient learning and an increase in overall productivity. If you're fond of constantly learning new skills and knowledge, you need to find an environment which has a continuous quality-improvement framework; learning and development policies and procedures are implemented and are a high priority in the organisation. Such organisations also see their employees as an investment, and training is an opportunity for both them and their employees to grow.

Motivation to Learn

Some people love and even crave learning anything and everything. If they recognise a deficiency in their knowledge, they're onto it. If they have to master something difficult, they see it as another challenge to overcome or a situation in which they can prove to themselves that they can do anything if they put their minds to. We've all met these people. So how do they remain so motivated to learn despite no monetary gain or physical rewards?

Well, these people implicitly enjoy learning. *Good for them,* you might be thinking. So, what about the rest who see learning new things as a hassle and are resistant to change? How do they become and remain motivated? There is no generic answer. Everyone is different, and it requires some self-reflection to discover how you can become motivated to learn.

Here are some suggestions to help those struggling with motivation to learn:

Recall a particular time when you were not motivated to learn something and procrastinated until you had no other choice but to learn it. For me, it was my times tables. To this day I still loathe mathematics and resist the need to learn new theorems. When I was in year two, I had to learn my times tables for homework over two weeks, as we were going to be tested in front of our classmates. For me, this was the worst thing ever: mathematics and talking in front of classmates I was not particularly fond of.

With fear of ridicule as my motivation, I set myself a task of memorising one number's set every day until I reached my twelve times tables. I told myself that if I made a mistake, I'd have to start my repetition from the beginning again. I can proudly say I still know my times tables. Fear of ridicule had motivated me to learn.

I also remember that once I had memorised my twos and threes, it was no longer that difficult. Since I had turned something hard into something easy, it started to become enjoyable. So overcoming another obstacle (another set of times tables) became the main form of motivation.

Now it's your turn. Uncover the main motivator in one of your own memories and whether this remained stable or changed as you began developing your skills and learning. Once you do this with one example, do it two more times. Is there a pattern? Are your motivating factors consistent over a variety of situations? If so, that is brilliant. Now you need to put yourself in a situation where this factor can be introduced and begin to take effect.

You may find that the motivating factor is solely dependent upon the situation. Your will to beat your class rival (competition) in an English test may not motivate you to reach first place in Ancient History, as your rival does not take that subject. Using this analogy, find a factor which will motivate you in your workplace. This factor must be positive and long lasting; it should not be based on a rival, as that person may leave your workplace unexpectedly, unravelling your motivation. Once you've found your factor, get yourself started and see if you become motivated.

Motivation to Work

Abraham Maslow suggested that our actions are motivated by satisfying certain needs, beginning with the physiological—from the bottom of the hierarchy to the top. As you move up the pyramid, the needs increase in complexity. If you incorporate your work into reaching self-actualisation in the sense of ambition—reaching a status in the social ladder or attaining a high reputation within a company—you can use your work to reach your self-actualisation goals.

Before you're able to progress up the levels of the pyramid, each deficiency must first be met in each level.

Maslow's Hierarchy of Needs

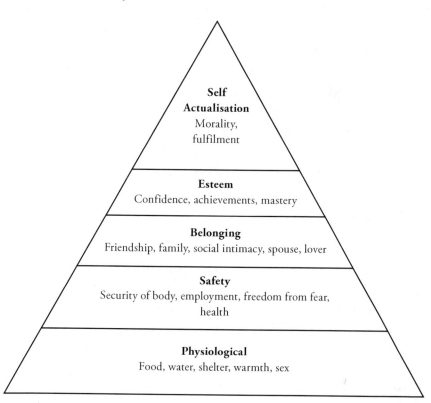

From using this pyramid, the theory indicates that you cannot reach the stage of belonging until you have satisfied your physiological and safety needs to a basic degree. Once your

Deficiency needs, such as food if you're hungry or attaining secure employment, are satisfied only then can you properly address or become motivated to satisfy your higher needs in the pyramid.

Maslow acknowledged that these levels are not followed exactly. For some people, attaining esteem within the workplace is more important than committing to a long-term relationship for intimacy. Regardless of who you are and what order these levels are for you, by understanding these needs, you can become more motivated and satisfied by the work you do.

By understanding your own personal order, you can focus your efforts on meeting those needs so you can climb the pyramid. This in itself should be motivating, as the rewards for becoming self-actualised are great. Overall, self-actualised people live a happier and more fulfilling life than their non-self-actualised counterparts. Self-actualised people have been found to possess the following attributes and behaviours:

- *Appreciation for the little things:* Self-actualised people take the time to enjoy life. You do not see them constantly rushing. They are the ones walking at a calm pace while they absorb their surroundings. From this they observe the wonders of nature, realise the world's complexities, and are thereby constantly reminded of their insignificance. This leaves them in a state of awe. It is the little things that bring them back to earth, and they appreciate life itself.
- *Realistic:* They have realistic perceptions of themselves, others, and their environment. They recognise their own faults and limitations when it comes to work performance, abilities, and personal attributes. Rather than accepting their faults, they actively seek ways to eradicate them, if possible. Their realism can be interpreted as pessimism, but this is a mistake. Self-actualised individuals are positive people who strive to make the world a better place by first looking inwards.
- *Problem solvers:* These use a proactive approach toward problems and do not stop until a solution is found. If they believe they have the personal capacity to make a difference, they do not hesitate as long as this difference will bring about resolution. They also have the wisdom to accept the problems they cannot solve or circumstances they cannot change, and so no longer expend energy on these problems.
- *Autonomous:* They do not like their identity or reputation to be intertwined with another individual or institution. They are their own being and exert a lot of effort into ensuring that their identity is autonomous.
- *A need for privacy:* Although self-actualised individuals are quite often gregarious, they need time-outs. They use these times to refuel and to reflect on what they have accomplished and where

they want to go in life. Some meditate or read. The aim of their privacy is to clear their minds and identify what parts of their lives are the most important and what areas they wish to develop.

- *Spontaneous:* Participating in unplanned activities or being met with an unforseen challenge is the spice of life. Although routine activities are enjoyable, being spontaneous or indulging impulses occasionally is also part of being self-actualised.

Now that you understand what it's like to be self-actualised, you can take a look at who you are as a person—in your private life, working life, or social life—and decide whether you're self-actualised. You may even begin to identify people who display these behaviours and attributes; notice that these people are successful or content. If you would like to reach this final state, you must first understand the order of your needs levels and the best ways to climb the pyramid. This in itself is self-motivating and should encourage you to become self-actualised in your working environment, as it occupies a large portion of your life.

Self-Efficacy and Motivation

As you might have gathered, motivation is a multidimensional concept. Many theories exist, all trying to explain how motivation enriches our lives in the workplace. Bandura's concept of self-efficacy overlaps with the idea of motivation in explaining how our beliefs about our competencies cripple our ability to become or to remain motivated.

Bandura's paper on self-efficacy has been referenced, discussed, and integrated into several psychologist's frameworks. These analysts all argue a unique interpretation of the term *self-efficacy.* For the purpose of this book, self-efficacy can be simply understood as the belief or confidence in one's ability to complete tasks, overcome obstacles, and instigate change.

When individuals believe they do not have the capacity to learn or to achieve their goals, their motivation is low. People who believe they are capable but lack the confidence to carry out a task require encouragement in order to be motivated. Those with high self-efficacy are generally self-driven and motivated to overcome new obstacles.

To broaden your understanding, below are examples of the behaviours of those with different levels of self-efficacy.

People with a strong sense of self-efficacy

- develop a deepened interest in areas they first believed were too challenging but then overcame;
- are highly committed to activities which they find enjoyable, challenging, or satisfying;
- use setbacks as an opportunity to learn and quickly approach the situation with a new strategy; and
- enjoy situations which involve challenges, as these are seen as times to demonstrate their competencies and abilities.

People with a low sense of self-efficacy

- are not motivated to solve problems or participate in challenging tasks;
- avoid challenging tasks due to a lack of confidence;
- believe failure to complete a difficult task is a platform for embarrassment, with their incompetence highlighted; and
- often lose confidence in their own abilities and self-worth, especially in the presence of others with a higher sense of self-efficacy.

As you can see, the behaviours of a person with low self-efficacy are significantly different from those of a person a with strong sense of self-efficacy. If you have low self-efficacy, do not lose heart. There are ways to change this. If you're not motivated to instigate change, perhaps you will be now that you know that it directly affects your ability to be motivated. Change can stop the vicious cycle.

For you to increase your self-efficacy and increase your ability to remain motivated, you must grasp how self-efficacy first develops. Once you understand this, you can actively seek out these factors so that your self-efficacy grows. Although self-efficacy develops throughout your childhood, it is not then set in stone. It can be moulded and continues to change throughout your life. According to Bandura, there are four main factors which develop self-efficacy:

- *Social modelling:* This is a form of vicarious learning; watching others whom we believe to be similar to us successfully complete a task makes us believe that we too can master that or a similar task.

- *Social persuasion:* Verbal encouragement from others when you are doubting yourself or struggling to complete a task persuades you that you are capable. This encouragement helps you attain a goal when you didn't believe you had the skills, knowledge, or competency.

- *Mastery experiences:* Bandura recognises mastery experiences as the most powerful factor in developing self-efficacy. Mastery experiences involve you succeeding in a task without social modelling or persuasion. By performing this task successfully, you strengthen your sense of self-efficacy. However, if you do not complete the task, this can be detrimental to that sense.

- *Psychological and physiological responses:* The physiological responses and cognitions we undergo as we experience new and challenging tasks can determine our sense of self-efficacy. For example, physiologically you experience your heart pounding, palms sweating, and nervousness as you sit for your final examination. You might interpret these responses as a sign of your own inadequacy. If you're also simultaneously thinking, *I'm going to fail* or *I'm too dumb to pass this exam*, these negative cognitions combined with your physiological responses lead to a severely reduced sense of self-efficacy when sitting for future examinations.

However, Bandura states that it is the intensity of these cognitions and responses rather than their interpretation which holds the most influence. By learning how to reduce your stress and substitute the negative cognitions with positive ones—*I can do this; this exam seems tough, but I'm going to try my best*—will slowly increase your sense of self-efficacy and prevent its reduction in similar circumstances.

With this understanding of the factors which help people develop their self-efficacy, what now? Well, you can start by putting yourself into situations in which these factors are replicated. You can begin by participating in an activity in which you have never been involved. This could be learning how to knit, playing an instrument, or running a 5K without stopping. Then set yourself goals to mark your progress and mastery of your chosen activity.

As you progress, you will develop your skills while also changing your perception of yourself; you will believe you are capable of completing difficult tasks. Starting with this situation, your newfound sense of self-efficacy can then be generalised to other aspects of your life. Once your sense becomes strong, you will become motivated to master other similar or new tasks to enhance your sense of self-efficacy. This has, in essence, turned your vicious cycle into a positive one; you have self-efficacy and motivation to complete harder tasks, leading to greater self-efficacy via mastery experiences and responses to more experiences.

Occupational Stress

At some point, everyone experiences occupational stress. This could be because you have just started a new job or your workload has just drastically increased. Whatever the reason, you need to develop a strategy to minimise and cope with stress.

Now ask yourself, *What are the top five factors which cause me stress?* Are there any ways you can minimise these stress triggers or eradicate them from your working environment? Below are some examples of common occupational stress triggers and suggested strategies for coping with and minimising stress.

Understaffing

When an organisation has fewer personnel than required to perform tasks or meet client requirements within a team, this places more pressure on individuals. They must work harder and longer to take up the slack for the absent team members. The amount of stress from understaffing can grow exponentially, especially if understaffing is not temporary due to slow or inactive recruitment and selection processes.

To minimise stress caused by understaffing, you need to communicate this issue to the rest of your team and your manager. Emphasise the amount of pressure distributed among you and the other team members and how you believe finding more staff is the appropriate corrective action.

The Boss or Upper Management

You can confront your boss and schedule a meeting to discuss any pressing issues you might have. It is best not to procrastinate on issues and let them proliferate. Addressing an issue directly is more effective than procrastinating; it is the first step to rectifying problems and alleviating your stress.

Need for Training

So you have been thrust into the deep end with no prior learning or training and feel as though you are expected to master your new set of responsibilities and tasks. What happens? You get stressed. If you believe you have some knowledge or skill gaps that will affect your ability to meet KPIs or targets or to perform your job competently, communicate these gaps to your manager or HR personnel. He or she will note the discussion, and if your performance is not up to par, he or she can recommend suitable training. Undergoing training or stating your need for training to managers or HR personnel is just one way to alleviate stress.

Ambiguous Job Role

This stressor is common in small organisations where job descriptions are not clearly outlined. Employees are confused about what constitutes their responsibilities and which tasks are priorities.

Long Travel Time

No one is exempt from experiencing stress when stuck in peak-hour traffic—not to mention when it is cold and raining and you need walk to your source of public transport. These factors all contribute to your level of occupational stress. When you're searching for a job, take them into account. Will you be able to handle the long travel time? Will this eventually be a determining factor in your decision to seek other employment?

Lack of Employee Trust

Being constantly micromanaged by your supervisor or manager is stressful. It is hard to maximise your productivity when you are worried about someone peeking behind your back and judging your work. One method of increasing trust is to communicate. Tell your direct supervisor of the tasks you will complete and when they will be completed. Also state that you will ask them for help if and when you need it. When you clarify this frequently, they should allow you more space to work independently and develop trust in you, thereby alleviating your stress.

Social Loafing

This is almost the opposite of understaffing. When there are too many staff with similar roles, everyone expects other members to work harder. As a consequence, a lot of staff members do not work to their full capacity, and the team collectively becomes less productive. This can also place a strain on employees with a hard work ethic; they continue to work just as hard as they were in a smaller team and feel as though they are taking up the slack. This is a common stress trigger in organisations.

An Unappreciative Boss

When you have an unappreciative boss, you may experience the following thoughts:

- My career progression, wants, and goals are invalid.
- I'm only there to clock in and clock out.

- I feel uncomfortable raising issues to management.
- I feel that the work I contribute is unrecognised and that I do not matter within a team.

It is hard to reduce the stress associated with an unappreciative boss. One solution is to start seeking alternative employment. You can also opt to transfer departments (if applicable). It is ultimately up to you to decide whether this factor is influential enough to make you leave your current organisation.

If you understand the major factors which cause you stress in your working environment, you can initiate strategies to combat them or manage them. However, certain levels of stress are necessary to reach optimum productivity. This is known as eustress.

Eustress is positive stress. It motivates you to continue working in difficult conditions and can provide a lot of enjoyment to those whom thrive on being challenged and productive.

	Low stress	*Medium-high stress*
Positive stress	Low performance	Optimum performance (medium stress)
Negative stress	Boredom	Burnout

The table above demonstrates that a fine balance must be found between having too much positive stress and not enough. Negative stress hinders performance, regardless of whether it is experienced at high or low levels. The definition of what is a high or low amount of stress varies among employees; some employees do not cope well under pressure, and any form of stress becomes a high level. Someone who copes well under high pressure may feel this as low level. The level of stress people experience is determined by their perception and stress thresholds, ultimately determining their optimum level of stress for high performance.

Generation Y and Upcoming Trends

Some major corporations have adopted organisational strategies that contrast the traditional HR view that corporations serve as a resource for career development with the view that employees serve as a resource for the organisation. This approach goes hand in hand with Generation Y's characteristics and approaches to careers. Current research indicates that Generation Y employees currently make up almost 20 per cent of the Australian workforce. Each generation has unique attributes which must be utilised to an organisation's advantage.

Gen Y is the most information technology and media literate generation in history. This attribute comes with the following trends:

- emphasis on experiential learning, activism, and practical learning;
- tailored training within an organisation;
- more mentoring and coaching;
- a need for immediate gratification; and
- customised career paths in which staying in one company is not expected and horizontal mobility in an organisation is exercised and career progression no longer depends upon occupying a managerial position.

	Before	**Present**
Career objective	Saving money for retirement.	Seeking purpose in work.
Most important needs	Appreciative boss.	Supportive colleagues. Appreciative boss. Suitable working conditions.
Working hours	Standard nine-to-five business hours.	Flexible working hours.
Preferred workplace	Office.	Anyplace that is safe and conducive to completing work.

Overall career	Have a stable career and be loyal to an organisation.	Try different career avenues. Stability means stagnation; best to keeping changing organisations or career climbing.
Promotions	Based on longevity; is more senior has the right to a promotion.	Based on skillset, experience, and notable achievements. Longevity in an organisation is not a valid justification for promotion.
Work ethic	Completing set tasks to the best of one's ability Working hard and respecting upper-management decisions.	Trying to make a unique mark or contribution—in their own organisation or business. Continual innovation.
	Before	**Present**
Training and development	Seen as an insult; you need to learn more in order to keep your job.	Seen as a positive and an opportunity to learn and grow skill sets and competencies. Employees request further training from employers. Training is a means of requesting more pay.
Pay scale	Believe pay rates should remain confidential and inaccessible to staff.	Believe in pay transparency; the organisation needs to justify why employees are paid at their given rates.

Employee Autonomy and decision making	Prefer upper management to make decisions. Worried about penalties for mistakes.	Enjoy the freedom to make decisions concerning own work responsibilities. Uses mistakes to learn and improve work productivity.
Community involvement	Is not essential for a business to function and retain customers; is done only if it is not a huge expense to the organisation.	Organisations with corporate social responsibility policies and procedures are respected and more desirable as an employer. Community involvement and volunteering is valued by employees.

These characteristics hint at the expectations Gen Yers have when they join the workforce. They believe that practical work experiences and project participation are more beneficial than traditional classroom training and simulations. They expect more on-the-job learning and many career progression opportunities.

Now, if you do belong to Gen Y, don't be offended when I say you expect too much. This is one of the major problems with Gen Y. When you graduate from university with a bachelor's or master's degree with little industry-related work experience, you cannot expect to be earning a lot of money. All the knowledge gained throughout your university experience is applicable in a work environment, but it is purely theoretical. There is a huge difference between learning theories and concepts from a textbook and working in a business environment.

Another point to consider is that every year there are thousands of graduates with the same level of education. You need to think what makes you more competitive than all these other candidates. It will not be how high your GPA is; it will be your work experience.

Changing Career Perspectives

With Generation Y eventually dominating the workforce, their different and even conflicting career perspectives will emerge within small and large organisations. Employers must be aware of how these new perspectives will impact their working culture and retention, and how employees will remain happy in their workplace.

Cross-Cultural Differences That Enhance Or Hinder an Application

When you're applying for jobs, it is imperative that you remain culturally sensitive. This means being sensitive to how the interviewers' culture influences the way they make judgements about you and the person they select, but also how your own culture influences how others perceive you and how you perceive others.

Individualistic vs. Collectivist Cultures

Psychologists have conducted numerous cross-cultural studies and have established two categories: collectivist and individualistic cultures. These categories are defined by certain characteristics and include certain nations. They also include characteristics which describe their associated personal attributes and attitudes expressed by the people, their behaviours, and their approach to their working lives.

Cultures described by psychologists as individualistic have the following characteristics:

- People are more concerned about themselves,; their career progression, what they want to achieve, and what they want does not involve others.
- Hiring and promotions are based on merit, and every customer and employee should be treated equally.
- Extraversion, confidence, and being self-driven are encouraged.
- Management involves managing employees behaviours.
- Individuals strive for their own progression rather than that of a group or organisation.

227

Collectivist cultures are very different from individualistic ones. The mindset is one of harmony and maintaining group cohesion in work environments and within social circles. In saying this, collectivist and individualistic cultures live by different and even clashing perspectives. The best way to demonstrate this is looking at their different perspectives on divorce:

Individualistic: "What does my heart say?"

Collectivist: "What will other people say?"

How these perspectives interplay within a work environment has been famously studied by many organisational psychologists. Hofstedes's dimension study is extensively referred to throughout the literature. This and other studies identify the following characteristics as collectivist:

- Individuals gain their sense of identity from their groups and social circles.
- Group cohesion is paramount.
- Individual achievements are not recognised without consideration of combined group efforts.
- Direct appraisals made by management are damaging to group harmony.
- Favoured customers and organisational members receive better treatment than others.
- Being humble and listening to others are endearing qualities, rather than speaking out and being extraverted.

As a collectivist in an individualistic nation such as Australia, you may find it difficult to land a job—not because you're not qualified or experienced, but because you struggle to sell yourself in an interview. You've been brought up with the principles of being humble, sharing your achievements amongst your colleagues, and letting your actions speak for themselves.

In present-day Australia this does not work. You are facing candidates who are just as qualified and experienced; all are fighting for one position. You need to show the interviewer that you're better than all of them. How can you do this if you're humble and downplay your achievements and experience? The answer is, you can't.

It will take a conscious effort to temporarily underdo years of cultural norming and not to do downplay yourself in a forty-five-minute interview. Being aware of these boundaries to success is the first step toward overcoming them. Seeking guidance, advice, or training can assist you in this process.

Top Ten FAQs from Clients

1. What is the difference between a CV and a résumé?

A CV is an abbreviation for *curriculum vitae,* a Latin term used to describe a summary of one's experiences and skills. CVs are most commonly longer than résumés and are used in industries such as medicine, academia, and education. They elaborate on academic background, any recent and notable publications, awards, significant achievements, and degrees.

A résumé is also a summary, although it is significantly shorter than a CV. Résumés highlight key words and skills that employers are seeking for a particular position and are specifically tailored to each application.

In this book, I have used the terms *CV* and *résumé* interchangeably in order to prevent confusion in my readers.

2. How long should my CV be?

The answer to this question is not simply two pages if you're a junior and up to six if you're a senior. The amount you should include in your CV depends upon the amount of experience and skills you have. If you're a junior with little experience, it is best to keep your CV short. You need to avoid the temptation to elevate or expand upon your experiences, as this can lead you into trouble.

If you have extensive experience, you should elaborate on the achievements you have made in each organisation and the key skills or competencies you have acquired. Focus mainly on the most recent three experiences you have, especially if your working history is quite extensive.

3. Can I change my job title on my CV?

It is highly recommended that you not elevate your job role or responsibilities to the point that they are fictitious. Changing your job title(s) is a derivative of fraud, and you will be caught when you reach the reference check stage.

4. Should I include referees?

This is a massive debate amongst HR professionals. Should you write, "References available upon request," or provide your referees straight out on your CV? I always advise my clients not to include referees on a CV. These are my reasons why:

- References should be used only at the end of the interview stage, when employers or consultants are conducting reference checks and are seriously considering providing you with a letter of offer.
- You do not want your referees to be contacted unless you have progressed to the final interview stage.
- Recruitment consultants especially are prone to harassing referees for references, as they cannot make a placement and thereby make their commission without a minimum of two solid reference checks.
- Your referees may opt out of providing a reference for you if they are constantly disturbed or called.

To be fair, the arguments other HR professionals offer are just as valid:

- Recruitment consultants or potential employers may interpret a lack of references on a CV as potential deception—that is, you have not really worked where you state you have worked.
- You have had confrontations or burned bridges with your previous employers and do not feel comfortable listing them as referees.

- You are making it harder for a recruitment consultant or employer to conduct reference checks, as they now have to seek out this information as opposed to it already being available on your CV.

With these two perspectives, you are now in the position to decide whether or not to include your referees on your CV.

5. Can I use a testimonial?

You sure can! Just like on LinkedIn, you can include testimonials from a supervisor or a colleague endorsing your skills, knowledge, and contributions. If you include a testimonial on your CV, make sure you have that person's permission first, as the testimonial may be tested during reference checks.

6. Do I ask about money in an interview?

Money is a sensitive topic to discuss during the interview stages. However, it is up to the individual candidate whether he or she feels the need to discuss the remuneration package or salary during the interview. I recommend that clients wait for the employer or its representatives to first mention money. You are welcome to take this approach on-board or take a different approach.

7. The more the better on my CV, right?

The best CVs are not determined by how long they are, but by their content and structure. The content needs to be concise and to demonstrate that you possess the hard skills necessary for the job you're applying to. Having long bullet-point lists of responsibilities or skills is not necessary. Your soft skills, such as in verbal communication and conflict resolution, will be tested in the interview stage. Allocate space for your technical skills and knowledge.

8. If they ask for my current boss's contact details for a reference check, should I give it to them, even though my boss and I do not get on?

Most recruitment consultants or employers contact the references you have provided on your CV. However, the recruitment consultant must abide by strict regulations—for instance, the references must be from two supervisors or managers within the last three years of employment, and they may request your current supervisor's details to meet this requirement. If this is the case, you can say that you will provide an alternative, as you do not want to alert your current boss that you are job hunting. Employers should respect and understand this reasoning and accept an alternative reference. Character references may be also acceptable.

9. Is there a faster way to get a job than applying and then waiting for them to call?

There are both proactive and passive job application strategies. Proactive strategies discussed in this book allow clients to secure a job more quickly than a passive approach. Although conducting follow-up calls and emails or seeking out positions in organisations with no advertisements can be quite daunting, having the confidence to use this strategy is rewarding. With the amount of competition Australians are facing, candidates who are enthusiastic and proactive will secure the job first.

10. Should I include my GPA?

Your GPA is not necessary on your CV unless it is a requirement for your application to be accepted. If it is required, include it. If your GPA is high or is at a level you're proud of, you should include it on your CV, next to your degree. (Include the mark you gained over the total possible mark.) If your GPA isn't as high as you'd hoped and is not required, you should not include it on your CV. Only add things on your CV which add value to an understanding of who you are as a worker.

RCI Success Feedback

On behalf of RCI Success, I hope the information provided in this book has exceeded your expectations. The goal is to teach you skills and knowledge which will benefit you not only now but also in the future.

Programs are available which cover the step-by-step breakdown of job application strategies, how recruitment agencies operate, and interview processes, including assessment centres and psychometric testing. I encourage you to utilise RCI Success services so you may secure a job quickly. These are available via the website: http://rcisuccess.com.au.

For other useful tips and interesting subject matter, visit my blog at http://rcisuccess.net.

I'd appreciate your feedback regarding this book. Please send your thoughts to info@rcisuccess.com.au with "Career Guidance for Now and for the Future" in the subject line. Alternatively, you can fill out RCI Success's online enquiry form with your comments via the website.

Thank you for using

RCIS

Resumés, Cover Letters & Interviews lead to Your SUCCESS

Bibliography

American Society on Aging and American Society of Consultant Pharmacists Foundation. "Facilitating Behavior Change." 2102. http://www.adultmeducation.com/FacilitatingBehaviorChange.html.

Advertising Standards Bureau. "Codes and Initiatives we administer." 2014. http://www.adstandards.com.au/advertisingstandards/codesweadminister.

Australian Competition & Consumer Commission. "Know Who You're Dealing With." SCAMwatch. 2014. http://www.scamwatch.gov.au/content/index.phtml/itemId/693900.

———. "Business." 2104. http://www.accc.gov.au/business.

Australian Department of Immigration and Border Protection. "Your Rights and Obligations—Immigration Facts for Workers." 2014. https://www.immi.gov.au/skilled/rights-obligations-workers.htm.

Australian Human Rights Commission. "A guide to Australia's anti-discrimination laws." 2007. https://www.humanrights.gov.au/guide-australias-anti-discrimination-laws.

Australian Taxation Office. "Australian Government." 2014. https://www.ato.gov.au/.

Bandura, A. "Self-efficacy: Toward a Unifying Theory of Behavioural Change." *Psychological Review* 84, no. 2 (1977): 191-215.

————. "Self-efficacy Mechanism in Human Agency." *American Psychologist* 37, no. 2 (1982): 122-47.

Binder, J., et al. "Human Brain Language Areas Identified by Functional Magnetic Resonance Imaging." *The Journal of Neuroscience* 17, no. 1 (1991): 353-62.

Clearly Business Enterprise Centre. "Supporting, Resourcing, Growing." 2014. http://www.sydneymetrobec.com.au/.

Commonwealth of Australia. "Identity Crime." 2014. http://www.afp.gov.au/policing/fraud/identity-crime.

Deakin University Australia Worldly. "STAR technique." 2014. http://www.deakin.edu.au/students/jobs-career/finding-jobs-and-applications/star-technique.

Deci, E., R. Koestner, and R. Ryan. "A Meta-Analytic Review of Experiments Examining the Effects of Extrinsic Rewards on Intrinsic Motivation." *Psychological Bulletin* 125, no. 6 (1999): 627-68.

Fair Work Ombudsman. "Australian Government: Fair Work Ombudsman." 2014. http://www.fairwork.gov.au/ending-employment/unfair-dismissal.

————. Australian Government. "Pay." 2014. http://www.fairwork.gov.au/pay.

————. "National Employment Standards." 2014. http://www.fairwork.gov.au/Employee-entitlements/national-employment-standards.

Free Dictionary, s.v. "ascending reticular activating system." http://medical-dictionary.thefreedictionary.com/ascending+reticular+activating+system.

Harkins, S. "Social loafing and Social Facilitation." *Journal of Experimental Social Psychology* 23, no. 1 (1987): 1-18.

Hofstede, G., and M. Bond. "Hofstede's Culture Dimensions: An Independent Validation Using Rokeach's Value Survey." *Journal of Cross-Cultural Psychology* 15, no. 4 (1984): 417-33.

Judge, T., D. Heller, and M. Mount. "Five-factor model of personality and job satisfaction: A meta-analysis." *Journal of Applied Psychology* 87, no. 3 (2002): 530-41.

Le Fevre, M., J. Matheny, and G. Kolt. (1986). "Eustress, distress, and interpretation in occupational stress." *Journal of Managerial Psychology* 18, no. 7 (1986): 726-44. doi:10.1108/02683940310502412.

Learning Marketing. "AIDA Communication Model." 2014. http://www. learnmarketing.net/aida.html.

Maslow, A. "'Higher' and 'Lower' Needs." *Journal of Psychology: Interdisciplinary and Applied* 25, no. 2 (1948): 433-36.

NSW Government: Lawlink Police & Justice. "Becoming a JP." 2013. http://www.jp.nsw.gov.au/jp/becomejp.html,c=y.

NSW Government: WorkCover. "Work Health and Safety." 2012. http:// www.workcover.nsw.gov.au/newlegislation2012/Pages/default.aspx.

Pepperdine University, Graziadio School of Business. "Describing Your Accomplishments." 2014. http://bschool.pepperdine.edu/career/content/ accomplishments.pdf.

Petty, R., J. Cacioppo, and D. Schumann. "Central and Peripheral Routes to Advertising Effectiveness: The Moderating Role of Involvement." *Journal of Consumer Research* 10 (1983): 135-46.

Psychology Glossary. "Behavioural Inhibition System." 2014. http:// www.psychology-lexicon.com/cms/glossary/glossary-b/1517-behavioral- inhibition-system.html.

Ryan, R., and E. Deci. "Intrinsic and Extrinsic Motivations: Classic Definitions and New Directions." *Contemporary Educational Psychology* 25 (2000): 54-67. http://mmrg.pbworks.com/f/Ryan,+Deci+00.pdf.

Terjesen, S., S. Viniicombe, and C. Freeman. "Attracting Generation Y graduates: Organisational attributes, likelihood to apply and sex difference." *International Journal of Career Management* 12, no. 6 (2007): 504-22.

Triandis, H. "Individualism-Collectivism and Personality." *Journal of Personality* 69, no. 6 (2013): 907-24.

University of Texas at Tyler: Office of Career Services. "Accomplishment Statements." 2104. http://www.uttyler.edu/careerservices/files/Accomp lishment%20Statements.pdf.

University of Western Australia. "Computer Workstation Ergonomics." 2013. http://www.safety.uwa.edu.au/health-wellbeing/physical/ergonomics/ workstation.